The Blockade of the Gaza Strip

Other Books of Related Interest

Opposing Viewpoints Series

Anti-Semitism
Israel
The Middle East Peace Process
Palestinian Territories

At Issue Series

Is Foreign Aid Necessary?
Should the US Close Its Borders?
What Is Humanity's Greatest Challenge?
What Role Should the US Play in the Middle East?

Current Controversies Series

Deporting Immigrants
The Middle East
Patriotism
Politics and Religion

"Congress shall make no law ... abridging the freedom of speech, or of the press."

First Amendment to the US Constitution

The basic foundation of our democracy is the First Amendment guarantee of freedom of expression. The Opposing Viewpoints series is dedicated to the concept of this basic freedom and the idea that it is more important to practice it than to enshrine it.

OPPOSING
VIEWPOINTS®
SERIES

The Blockade of the Gaza Strip

Martin Gitlin, Book Editor

GREENHAVEN
PUBLISHING

Published in 2020 by Greenhaven Publishing, LLC
353 3rd Avenue, Suite 255, New York, NY 10010

Cover credit: Said Khatib/AFP/Getty Images

Cataloging-in-Publication Data

Names: Gitlin, Martin, editor.
Title: The blockade of the Gaza Strip / edited by Martin Gitlin.
Description: New York : Greenhaven Publishing, 2020. | Series: Opposing viewpoints | Includes
  bibliographical references and index. | Audience: Grades 9-12.
Identifiers: LCCN ISBN 9781534505087 (library bound) | ISBN 9781534505094 (pbk.)
Subjects: LCSH: Blockade--Gaza Strip. | Arab-Israeli conflict. | Arab-Israeli conflict--1993---
  Blockades | .Arab-Israeli conflict -- 1993- -- Peace.
Classification: LCC DS110.G3 B563 2020 | DDC 956.04--dc23

Manufactured in the United States of America

Website: http://greenhavenpublishing.com

Contents

Chapter 3: Is the Blockade of the Gaza Strip Inhumane?

Chapter 4: Can the Problem Be Solved?

The Importance of Opposing Viewpoints

P erhaps every generation experiences a period in time in which
the populace seems especially polarized, starkly divided on
the important issues of the day and gravitating toward the far ends
of the political spectrum and away from a consensus-facilitating
middle ground. The world that today's students are growing up in
and that they will soon enter into as active and engaged citizens
is deeply fragmented in just this way. Issues relating to terrorism,
immigration, women's rights, minority rights, race relations, health
care, taxation, wealth and poverty, the environment, policing,
military intervention, the proper role of government—in some
ways, perennial issues that are freshly and uniquely urgent and
vital with each new generation—are currently roiling the world.

If we are to foster a knowledgeable, responsible, active, and
engaged citizenry among today's youth, we must provide them
with the intellectual, interpretive, and critical-thinking tools and
experience necessary to make sense of the world around them and
of the all-important debates and arguments that inform it. After all,
the outcome of these debates will in large measure determine the
future course, prospects, and outcomes of the world and its peoples,
particularly its youth. If they are to become successful members
of society and productive and informed citizens, students need to
learn how to evaluate the strengths and weaknesses of someone
else's arguments, how to sift fact from opinion and fallacy, and
how to test the relative merits and validity of their own opinions
against the known facts and the best possible available information.
The landmark series Opposing Viewpoints has been providing
students with just such critical-thinking skills and exposure to the
debates surrounding society's most urgent contemporary issues
for many years, and it continues to serve this essential role with
undiminished commitment, care, and rigor.

The key to the series' success in achieving its goal of sharpening
students' critical-thinking and analytic skills resides in its title—

Opposing Viewpoints. In every intriguing, compelling, and engaging volume of this series, readers are presented with the widest possible spectrum of distinct viewpoints, expert opinions, and informed argumentation and commentary, supplied by some of today's leading academics, thinkers, analysts, politicians, policy makers, economists, activists, change agents, and advocates. Every opinion and argument anthologized here is presented objectively and accorded respect. There is no editorializing in any introductory text or in the arrangement and order of the pieces. No piece is included as a "straw man," an easy ideological target for cheap point-scoring. As wide and inclusive a range of viewpoints as possible is offered, with no privileging of one particular political ideology or cultural perspective over another. It is left to each individual reader to evaluate the relative merits of each argument—as he or she sees it, and with the use of ever-growing critical-thinking skills—and grapple with his or her own assumptions, beliefs, and perspectives to determine how convincing or successful any given argument is and how the reader's own stance on the issue may be modified or altered in response to it.

This process is facilitated and supported by volume, chapter, and selection introductions that provide readers with the essential context they need to begin engaging with the spotlighted issues, with the debates surrounding them, and with their own perhaps shifting or nascent opinions on them. In addition, guided reading and discussion questions encourage readers to determine the authors' point of view and purpose, interrogate and analyze the various arguments and their rhetoric and structure, evaluate the arguments' strengths and weaknesses, test their claims against available facts and evidence, judge the validity of the reasoning, and bring into clearer, sharper focus the reader's own beliefs and conclusions and how they may differ from or align with those in the collection or those of their classmates.

Research has shown that reading comprehension skills improve dramatically when students are provided with compelling, intriguing, and relevant "discussable" texts. The subject matter of these collections could not be more compelling, intriguing, or urgently relevant to today's students and the world they are poised to inherit. The anthologized articles and the reading and discussion questions that are included with them also provide the basis for stimulating, lively, and passionate classroom debates. Students who are compelled to anticipate objections to their own argument and identify the flaws in those of an opponent read more carefully, think more critically, and steep themselves in relevant context, facts, and information more thoroughly. In short, using discussable text of the kind provided by every single volume in the Opposing Viewpoints series encourages close reading, facilitates reading comprehension, fosters research, strengthens critical thinking, and greatly enlivens and energizes classroom discussion and participation. The entire learning process is deepened, extended, and strengthened.

For all of these reasons, Opposing Viewpoints continues to be exactly the right resource at exactly the right time—when we most need to provide readers with the critical-thinking tools and skills that will not only serve them well in school but also in their careers and their daily lives as decision-making family members, community members, and citizens. This series encourages respectful engagement with and analysis of opposing viewpoints and fosters a resulting increase in the strength and rigor of one's own opinions and stances. As such, it helps make readers "future ready," and that readiness will pay rich dividends for the readers themselves, for the citizenry, for our society, and for the world at large.

Introduction

> *"Israel regarded from the very beginning any wish to end the occupation—whether expressed peacefully or through struggle—as terrorism. From the beginning, it reacted brutally by collectively punishing the population for any demonstration of resistance."*
>
> *– Historian and social critic Noam Chomsky on Israeli treatment of Palestinians*

It doesn't take a serious history buff to understand that the basis of all military actions perpetrated by the government of Israel since the country was established in 1948 has been security. Through the ages the Jewish people have been harassed, chased, banished, and, most horrifying, killed for no other reason than their religion. Such was the case of the Holocaust (1941-1945), when six million were murdered systematically in an attempt to wipe out the Jewish population of Europe. It was that unforgettable event that inspired the formation of the Jewish state in the Middle East.

Israel has sought to justify all militancy over its seventy-year existence by the threats imposed by its neighbors. The latest pressure has been imposed by Hamas, which won Palestinian elections in 2006 and became what many believe is a threat to the very existence of Israel. Hamas refused to agree to the condition of continued aid to the Palestinians, including recognition of Israel as a nation, the rejection of violence, and the acceptance of previous agreements between its government and the Palestinian Authority.

Hamas soon took over Gaza. Under the hardline government led by Benjamin Netanyahu, the Israelis responded in 2007 with a land, sea, and air blockade of the Gaza Strip that some perceive as an occupation.

Israel has claimed that the blockade was necessary as a protection against terrorism, rocket attacks, or any other violent actions. It further contended that such action was needed to prevent weapons from falling into the hands of those that wished the country harm. And though it was understood that the blockade violated obligations to the Palestinian people based on previous ceasefire agreements, the Israeli government expressed the belief that it had no choice.

Though the Israeli government denies that the effect of its action has reached such a level, most consider the results of the blockade to be a humanitarian crisis. The World Bank reported in 2015 that nearly half of all Gaza residents were living in poverty.

Israel has continued to blame Hamas throughout. Indeed, the political group that controls Gaza has continued its terrorist attacks with rockets and mortars, though Israel has also been cited as a provocateur. The Israeli government also has pushed back against claims that it has created a humanitarian calamity, stating that it is Hamas that boasts full control over the Gaza Strip and has often diverted aid such as medical supplies to the area. Included was the seizing of two hundred tons of food delivered by the United Nations Relief and Works Agency (UNRWA). Israel has charged that even the Palestinian Authority has criticized Hamas for actions that threaten the well-being of Gazans, claiming that Hamas stole thousands of liters of fuel from local Gazan companies and that Israel had caused a fuel shortage.

Israel maintains it has attempted to mitigate suffering, citing a donation of $1 million in medical and humanitarian aid to the Gaza Strip in 2009 and caring for injured Palestinians in Israeli hospitals. Israel furthered asserted that it dispatched humanitarian aid to Gaza after a rocket attack against the country in 2014 provoked retaliation.

Some believe the entire problem stems from the continued refusal of Israel to recognize a Palestinian state and its general mistreatment of the Palestinian people. They offer that the blockade of the Gaza Strip is further evidence of that mistreatment. Some laud Hamas for what they perceive as protection from Israeli aggression and their desire to protect Palestinian rights.

The refusal of either side to budge has resulted in a blockade standoff that has extended into a second decade with no end in sight. The pro-Israeli faction believes that the blockade will be justified as long as Hamas controls Gaza and remains committed to bringing down the Jewish state. Those that rail against the blockade—even those that believe in the right of Israel to exist—claim that the blockade must be lifted for the standoff to end and progress to be made toward peace in the Middle East.

The blockade has inspired violent protests by Palestinians against what they deem to be Israeli occupation of their lands. The result has often been the deaths of some in the Israeli military, but mostly of Palestinian citizens. Nothing that has occurred since the blockade began suggests that such tragedy will not happen again.

There seems to be little hope based on rhetoric that two factions with militant leadership—Hamas on one side and a right-wing Netanyahu on the other—will ever come together to create a peaceful solution. A two-state solution in which the Palestinians can form their own nation and government seems quite unlikely unless iron-clad assurance of Israeli sovereignty can be negotiated. One would have to blink first.

In *Opposing Viewpoints: The Blockade of the Gaza Strip* authors explore the situation in chapters entitled "Is the Blockade of the Gaza Strip an Act of Aggression or Preservation of a Nation?," "Is the Blockade of the Gaza Strip Legal?," "Is the Blockade of the Gaza Strip Inhumane?," and "How Can the Problem Be Solved?" The shame of it all is that most Israelis and most Palestinians simply yearn to live in peace and prosperity. That has not happened over seven decades of Israeli existence. It seems as unlikely to happen as ever considering the current conditions.

OPPOSING
VIEWPOINTS®
SERIES

Is the Blockade of the Gaza Strip an Act of Aggression or Preservation of a Nation?

Chapter Preface

T he line is sometimes so fine between right and wrong that it is nearly invisible. Such is the reality regarding Israeli intent and action as the government seeks to ensure its existence for centuries to come.

What most folks agree is that indeed Israel has a right to exist. The Jewish people have been persecuted long and strongly enough since they began walking the Earth to justify the right to a nation of their own. But at what price? Many believe that Israel is persecuting the Palestinian people in the process of fighting against the threat of their own persecution.

Israel's blockade of the Gaza Strip is a complex issue, which comes as little surprise given the fact that peace in the Middle East has proven to be among the thorniest problems in the world for generations. It has led to many questions and no answers that can be universally embraced as viable. Those that back the blockade claim that it keeps weapons out of the hands of Hamas, which has stated its intention to wipe Israel off the map. That is a valid point. Those that rail against the blockade state that it has led to a humanitarian crisis for the Palestinian people. That too is a valid point. There is enough gray area to fill the sky.

This chapter will explore the fundamental questions of right and wrong. The opinions expressed in the following articles run the gamut from complete justification of the Israel blockade to the view that it is a moral outrage. But opinions are opinions for a reason. They are often not formed with objectivity. Those that back the blockade do not always delve into the humanitarian issue. And those that decry the blockade rarely explore the need for the protection of Israel. Readers must sift through the views expressed here to make their own judgments.

> *"If we do lift that blockade, it is patently obvious, Hamas will immediately bring in more of the weaponry it needs in order to pursue its declared goal of destroying us."*

Israel Is Protecting Itself Against Its Evil Next-Door Neighbor

David Horovitz

In the following viewpoint David Horovitz argues that Hamas has proven it can't be trusted and that therefore the blockade of Gaza is justified. In comparing Hamas to a dangerous neighbor the author further contends that lifting the blockade would result in weapons and ammunition entering its controlled area that he believes would certainly be used against Israel. He argues that, after all, Hamas has clearly stated its intention of destroying the Jewish state and has given no reason to believe that ending the blockade would weaken its resolve. Horovitz is the founding editor of the Times of Israel.

"Hamas, the Murderous Neighbor That Demands Israel Give It the Gun," by David Horovitz, *Times of Israel*, July 26, 2018. Reprinted by permission.

As you read, consider the following questions:

1. What are the feelings of the author about the intentions of Hamas?
2. Are there any solutions beyond maintaining the blockade that the author suggests to create peace?
3. How does the author use an analogy to make his point?

A few years ago, an awful new neighbor moved in next door. An ex-murderer, unreformed.

Life became a nightmare. He claimed we were on his land. We weren't. There'd been a dispute before he arrived, but we'd actually conceded.

He vowed alternately to force us out of the neighborhood and to kill us. He told anyone who'd listen that we had no right to be here and that he hated us. Unbelievably, some of the other neighbors supported him.

There were fights at the fence. We were scared to go outside. Life became a nightmare.

He tried to get a gun. He had friends who we knew would give him one. He said that if we didn't let him get the gun, he'd keep on harassing and attacking us.

So we said okay. We let him get the gun. He killed us.

That ridiculous story is essentially the tale of what's going on between Hamas and Israel. Except for the last part. That's not going to happen.

Hamas, a murderous Islamist terror organization, took violent control of the Gaza Strip in 2007, ousting Mahmoud Abbas's Palestinian Authority in a bloody coup.

Israel had unilaterally withdrawn two years earlier to the ostensibly undisputed pre-1967 lines—removing 7,000-8,000 civilians, pulling out the army.

Ever since, Hamas has made life as hellish for Israel as it possibly can—firing thousands of rockets indiscriminately into Israel, digging attack tunnels under the border, killing and wounding soldiers at the border fence, carrying out suicide bombings and other acts of terrorism, and most recently flying arson devices — kites and balloons—across the border to burn our lands.

All the while, in its guiding charter and in the speeches and propaganda of its leaders, it's told anybody who'll listen that it is bent on destroying Israel, that the Jews have no right to be here— or anywhere else for that matter—and that, sooner or later, it will wipe us out.

It's also been complaining to anyone who'll listen about the blockade that Israel (and Egypt) impose on the territory it controls. If we don't lift that blockade, it threatens, it'll keep on attacking us.

If we do lift that blockade, it is patently obvious, Hamas will immediately bring in more of the weaponry it needs in order to pursue its declared goal of destroying us. Nonetheless, quite astonishingly, various UN bodies, human rights groups, Turkish presidents, Swedish and Irish politicians, British opposition leaders, American presidential candidates, and other experts argue that Israel should indeed ease the restrictions on access it imposes on Gaza — that is, that Israel should indeed cooperate in the intended orchestration of its own destruction.

Of late, this ridiculous saga has been playing out with some mildly fresh but routinely disingenuous twists. For weeks, Hamas has been mobilizing the Gaza masses to hold protests at the border, with numerous attempts to damage and break through the fence, again in the publicly stated cause of "erasing" the border, flooding Israel with millions of Palestinians, and thus destroying the Jewish state. Defending that border, the Israeli army has killed some 140 people—dozens of them Hamas members. Was live fire necessary in each and every such case? It's hard to tell; abuses of open-fire regulations must be investigated. Nobody would be dead, however, were it not for the Hamas-instigated violence.

And in the past few days, Hamas has introduced a new tactic. It encourages young Gazans to protest at the fence, drawing Israeli army patrols, and then its snipers open fire on the soldiers. That's how Staff Sgt. Aviv Levi was killed on Friday, Israeli military officials say, and that's how a second soldier, now recovering in the hospital, was badly injured on Wednesday evening.

Later Wednesday, Israel hit back at Hamas in retaliation for the sniper fire, and killed three of its terrorists. In the absurd Hamas narrative, the Israeli response to its crime is unacceptable. And therefore, Hamas has placed its forces on alert and is, as ever, vowing revenge.

For all its relentless viciousness and cynical abuse of its own people, its misrepresentation of divine will and its sanctification of death, Hamas will never prevail. Utterly, insistently blind to any notion of Jewish sovereign legitimacy, it follows bloody, brutal but ultimately dunderheaded tactics in support of its foul and genocidal strategy.

Obviously, Israel is going to defend its border against terrorist attack. Obviously, Israel is going to retaliate when it comes under assault. And obviously, Israel is not going to lift the security blockade it imposes on Gaza so long as Hamas runs the Strip.

But, Hamas, overflowing with hatred for Israel, will not acknowledge the grimly farcical nature of its demand. Lift the blockade, or we'll hurt you more, it threatens. Lift the blockade, so that we can import the tools to hurt you more, it vows.

No.

And so the violence goes on, in one or other iteration.

Shame on the fools who buy into the Hamas narrative. And more shame on the Israel-haters who promote the Hamas agenda while understanding exactly what's going on.

Israel is not going to hand a gun to the murderer next door. What it could use is some help, support and understanding in trying to run the murderer out of town.

"*In early 2004, shortly before he
was assassinated by Israel, Hamas
founder Sheik Ahmed Yassin
said that Hamas could accept a
Palestinian state alongside Israel.
Hamas has since repeatedly
reiterated its willingness to accept a
two-state solution.*"

A Pervasive Mythology Obfuscates the Truth About Israel and Palestine

Jeremy R. Hammond

*In the following viewpoint Jeremy R. Hammond asserts that the
Israeli government was unwarranted in flexing its muscles through
a blockade of the Gaza Strip. Hammond uses both history and a
reflection on modern times to list ten myths about Israeli security
and threats from those that share the region. The author also touches
upon Biblical myths to make his point that Israel and its government
is to blame for the continued tension and dangerous situation in
the Middle East. Hammond is an independent journalist, political
analyst, and author.*

"Top Ten Myths about the Israeli-Palestinian Conflict", by Jeremy R. Hammond, *Foreign Policy Journal*. June 17, 2010. Reprinted by permission.

As you read, consider the following questions:

1. Did the author make provable points to legitimize his assertions that the myths he listed were not true?
2. Which of the myths offered in the viewpoint could be the most strongly argued against?
3. Does the author note any reason why so many myths have been placed into the public sphere?

A proper understanding of the Israeli-Palestinian conflict requires exposing numerous myths about its origins and the reasons it persists.

Myth #1—Jews and Arabs have always been in conflict in the region.

Although Arabs were a majority in Palestine prior to the creation of the state of Israel, there had always been a Jewish population, as well. For the most part, Jewish Palestinians got along with their Arab neighbors. This began to change with the onset of the Zionist movement, because the Zionists rejected the right of the Palestinians to self-determination and wanted Palestine for their own, to create a "Jewish State" in a region where Arabs were the majority and owned most of the land.

For instance, after a series of riots in Jaffa in 1921 resulting in the deaths of 47 Jews and 48 Arabs, the occupying British held a commission of inquiry, which reported their finding that "there is no inherent anti-Semitism in the country, racial or religious." Rather, Arab attacks on Jewish communities were the result of Arab fears about the stated goal of the Zionists to take over the land.

After major violence again erupted in 1929, the British Shaw Commission report noted that "In less than 10 years three serious attacks have been made by Arabs on Jews. For 80 years before the first of these attacks there is no recorded instance of any similar incidents." Representatives from all sides of the emerging conflict testified to the commission that prior to the First World War, "the Jews and Arabs lived side by side if not in amity, at least with tolerance, a quality which today is almost unknown in Palestine." The problem was that "The Arab people of Palestine are today united in their demand for representative government", but were being denied that right by the Zionists and their British benefactors.

The British Hope-Simpson report of 1930 similarly noted that Jewish residents of non-Zionist communities in Palestine enjoyed friendship with their Arab neighbors. "It is quite a common sight to see an Arab sitting in the verandah of a Jewish house", the report noted. "The position is entirely different in the Zionist colonies."

Myth #2—The United Nations created Israel.

The U.N. became involved when the British sought to wash its hands of the volatile situation its policies had helped to create, and to extricate itself from Palestine. To that end, they requested that the U.N. take up the matter.

As a result, a U.N. Special Commission on Palestine (UNSCOP) was created to examine the issue and offer its recommendation on how to resolve the conflict. UNSCOP contained no representatives from any Arab country and in the end issued a report that explicitly rejected the right of the Palestinians to self-determination. Rejecting the democratic solution to the conflict, UNSCOP instead proposed that Palestine be partitioned into two states: one Arab and one Jewish.

The U.N. General Assembly endorsed UNSCOP's in its Resolution 181. It is often claimed that this resolution "partitioned" Palestine, or that it provided Zionist leaders with a legal mandate for their subsequent declaration of the existence of the state of Israel, or some other similar variation on the theme. All such claims are absolutely false.

Resolution 181 merely endorsed UNSCOP's report and conclusions as a recommendation. Needless to say, for Palestine to have been officially partitioned, this recommendation would have had to have been accepted by both Jews and Arabs, which it was not.

Moreover, General Assembly resolutions are not considered legally binding (only Security Council resolutions are). And, furthermore, the U.N. would have had no authority to take land from one people and hand it over to another, and any such resolution seeking to so partition Palestine would have been null and void, anyway.

Myth #3—The Arabs missed an opportunity to have their own state in 1947.

The U.N. recommendation to partition Palestine was rejected by the Arabs. Many commentators today point to this rejection as constituting a missed "opportunity" for the Arabs to have had their own state. But characterizing this as an "opportunity" for the Arabs is patently ridiculous. The Partition plan was in no way, shape, or form an "opportunity" for the Arabs.

First of all, as already noted, Arabs were a large majority in Palestine at the time, with Jews making up about a third of the population by then, due to massive immigration of Jews from Europe (in 1922, by contrast, a British census showed that Jews represented only about 11 percent of the population).

Additionally, land ownership statistics from 1945 showed that Arabs owned more land than Jews in every single district of Palestine, including Jaffa, where Arabs owned 47 percent of the land while Jews owned 39 percent – and Jaffa boasted the highest percentage of Jewish-owned land of any district. In other districts, Arabs owned an even larger portion of the land. At the extreme other end, for instance, in Ramallah, Arabs owned 99 percent of the land. In the whole of Palestine, Arabs owned 85 percent of the land, while Jews owned less than 7 percent, which remained the case up until the time of Israel's creation.

Yet, despite these facts, the U.N. partition recommendation had called for more than half of the land of Palestine to be given to the Zionists for their "Jewish State". The truth is that no Arab could be reasonably expected to accept such an unjust proposal. For political commentators today to describe the Arabs' refusal to accept a recommendation that their land be taken away from them, premised upon the explicit rejection of their right to self-determination, as a "missed opportunity" represents either an astounding ignorance of the roots of the conflict or an unwillingness to look honestly at its history.

It should also be noted that the partition plan was also rejected by many Zionist leaders. Among those who supported the idea, which included David Ben-Gurion, their reasoning was that this would be a pragmatic step towards their goal of acquiring the whole of Palestine for a "Jewish State"—something which could be finally accomplished later through force of arms.

When the idea of partition was first raised years earlier, for instance, Ben-Gurion had written that "after we become a strong force, as the result of the creation of a state, we shall abolish partition and expand to the whole of Palestine." Partition should be accepted, he argued, "to prepare the ground for our expansion into the whole of Palestine." The Jewish State would then "have to preserve order," if the Arabs would not acquiesce, "by machine guns, if necessary."

Myth #4—Israel has a "right to exist".

The fact that this term is used exclusively with regard to Israel is instructive as to its legitimacy, as is the fact that the demand is placed upon Palestinians to recognize Israel's "right to exist", while no similar demand is placed upon Israelis to recognize the "right to exist" of a Palestinian state.

Nations don't have rights, people do. The proper framework for discussion is within that of the right of all peoples to self-determination. Seen in this, the proper framework, it is an elementary observation that it is not the Arabs which have denied Jews that right, but the Jews which have denied that right to the Arabs. The terminology of Israel's "right to exist" is constantly employed to obfuscate that fact.

As already noted, Israel was not created by the U.N., but came into being on May 14, 1948, when the Zionist leadership unilaterally, and with no legal authority, declared Israel's existence, with no specification as to the extent of the new state's borders. In a moment, the Zionists had declared that Arabs no longer the owners of their land – it now belonged to the Jews. In an instant, the Zionists had declared that the majority Arabs of Palestine were now second-class citizens in the new "Jewish State."

The Arabs, needless to say, did not passively accept this development, and neighboring Arab countries declared war on the Zionist regime in order to prevent such a grave injustice against the majority inhabitants of Palestine.

It must be emphasized that the Zionists had no right to most of the land they declared as part of Israel, while the Arabs did. This war, therefore, was not, as is commonly asserted in mainstream commentary, an act of aggression by the Arab states against Israel. Rather, the Arabs were acting in defense of their rights, to prevent the Zionists from illegally and unjustly taking over Arab lands and otherwise disenfranchising the Arab population. The act of aggression was the Zionist leadership's unilateral declaration of the existence of Israel, and the Zionists' use of violence to enforce their aims both prior to and subsequent to that declaration.

In the course of the war that ensued, Israel implemented a policy of ethnic cleansing. 700,000 Arab Palestinians were either forced from their homes or fled out of fear of further massacres, such as had occurred in the village of Deir Yassin shortly before the Zionist declaration. These Palestinians have never been allowed to return to their homes and land, despite it being internationally recognized and encoded in international law that such refugees have an inherent "right of return."

Palestinians will never agree to the demand made of them by Israel and its main benefactor, the U.S., to recognize Israel's "right to exist." To do so is effectively to claim that Israel had a "right" to take Arab land, while Arabs had no right to their own land. It is effectively to claim that Israel had a "right" to ethnically cleanse Palestine, while Arabs had no right to life, liberty, and the pursuit of happiness in their own homes, on their own land.

The constant use of the term "right to exist" in discourse today serves one specific purpose: It is designed to obfuscate the reality that it is the Jews that have denied the Arab right to self-determination, and not vice versa, and to otherwise attempt to legitimize Israeli crimes against the Palestinians, both historical and contemporary.

Myth #5—The Arab nations threatened Israel with annihilation in 1967 and 1973

The fact of the matter is that it was Israel that fired the first shot of the "Six Day War". Early on the morning of June 5, Israel launched fighters in a surprise attack on Egypt (then the United Arab Republic), and successfully decimated the Egyptian air force while most of its planes were still on the ground.

It is virtually obligatory for this attack to be described by commentators today as "preemptive". But to have been "preemptive", by definition, there must have been an imminent threat of Egyptian aggression against Israel. Yet there was none.

It is commonly claimed that President Nasser's bellicose rhetoric, blockade of the Straits of Tiran, movement of troops into the Sinai Peninsula, and expulsion of U.N. peacekeeping forces from its side of the border collectively constituted such an imminent threat.

Yet, both U.S. and Israeli intelligence assessed at the time that the likelihood Nasser would actually attack was low. The CIA assessed that Israel had overwhelming superiority in force of arms, and would, in the event of a war, defeat the Arab forces within two weeks; within a week if Israel attacked first, which is what actually occurred.

It must be kept in mind that Egypt had been the victim of aggression by the British, French, and Israelis in the 1956 "Suez Crisis", following Egypt's nationalization of the Suez Canal. In that war, the three aggressor nations conspired to wage war upon Egypt, which resulted in an Israeli occupation of the Sinai Peninsula. Under U.S. pressure, Israel withdrew from the Sinai in 1957, but Egypt had not forgotten the Israeli aggression.

Moreover, Egypt had formed a loose alliance with Syria and Jordan, with each pledging to come to the aid of the others in the event of a war with Israel. Jordan had criticized Nasser for not living up to that pledge after the Israeli attack on West Bank village of Samu the year before, and his rhetoric was a transparent attempt to regain face in the Arab world.

That Nasser's positioning was defensive, rather than projecting an intention to wage an offensive against Israel, was well recognized among prominent Israelis. As Avraham Sela of the Shalem Center has observed, "The Egyptian buildup in Sinai lacked a clear offensive plan, and Nasser's defensive instructions explicitly assumed an Israeli first strike."

Israeli Prime Minister Menachem Begin acknowledged that "In June 1967, we again had a choice. The Egyptian army concentrations in the Sinai approaches do not prove that Nasser was really about to attack us. We must be honest with ourselves. We decided to attack him."

Yitzhak Rabin, who would also later become Prime Minister of Israel, admitted in 1968 that "I do not think Nasser wanted war. The two divisions he sent to the Sinai would not have been sufficient to launch an offensive war. He knew it and we knew it."

Israelis have also acknowledged that their own rhetoric at the time about the "threat" of "annihilation" from the Arab states was pure propaganda.

General Chaim Herzog, commanding general and first military governor of the occupied West Bank following the war, admitted that "There was no danger of annihilation. Israeli headquarters never believed in this danger."

General Ezer Weizman similarly said, "There was never a danger of extermination. This hypothesis had never been considered in any serious meeting."

Chief of Staff Haim Bar-Lev acknowledged, "We were not threatened with genocide on the eve of the Six-Day War, and we had never thought of such possibility."

Israeli Minister of Housing Mordechai Bentov has also acknowledged that "The entire story of the danger of extermination was invented in every detail, and exaggerated a posteriori to justify the annexation of new Arab territory."

In 1973, in what Israelis call the "Yom Kippur War", Egypt and Syria launched a surprise offensive to retake the Sinai and the Golan Heights, respectively. This joint action is popularly described in contemporaneous accounts as an "invasion" of or act of "aggression" against Israel.

Yet, as already noted, following the June '67 war, the U.N. Security Council passed resolution 242 calling upon Israel to withdraw from the occupied territories. Israel, needless to say, refused to do so and has remained in perpetual violation of international law ever since.

During the 1973 war, Egypt and Syria thus "invaded" their own territory, then under illegal occupation by Israel. The corollary of the description of this war as an act of Arab aggression implicitly assumes that the Sinai Peninsula, Golan Heights, West Bank, and Gaza Strip were Israeli territory. This is, needless to say, a grossly false assumption that demonstrates the absolutely prejudicial and biased nature of mainstream commentary when it comes to the Israeli-Arab conflict.

This false narrative fits in with the larger overall narrative, equally fallacious, of Israeli as the "victim" of Arab intransigence and aggression. This narrative, largely unquestioned in the West, flips reality on its head.

Myth #6—U.N. Security Council Resolution 242 called only for a partial Israeli withdrawal.

Resolution 242 was passed in the wake of the June '67 war and called for the "Withdrawal of Israel armed forces from territories occupied in the recent conflict." While the above argument enjoys widespread popularity, it has no merit whatsoever.

The central thesis of this argument is that the absence of the word "the" before "occupied territories" in that clause means not "all of the occupied territories" were intended. Essentially, this argument rests upon the ridiculous logic that because the word "the" was omitted from the clause, we may therefore understand this to mean that "some of the occupied territories" was the intended meaning.

Grammatically, the absence of the word "the" has no effect on the meaning of this clause, which refers to "territories", plural. A simple litmus test question is: Is it territory that was occupied by Israel in the '67 war? If yes, then, under international law and Resolution 242, Israel is required to withdraw from that territory. Such territories include the Syrian Golan Heights, the West Bank, and the Gaza Strip.

The French version of the resolution, equally authentic as the English, contains the definite article, and a majority of the members of the Security Council made clear during deliberations that their understanding of the resolution was that it would require Israel to fully withdraw from all occupied territories.

Additionally, it is impossible to reconcile with the principle of international law cited in the preamble to the resolution, of "the inadmissibility of the acquisition of territory by war". To say that the U.N. intended that Israel could retain some of the territory it occupied during the war would fly in the face of this cited principle.

One could go on to address various other logical fallacies associated with this frivolous argument, but as it is absurd on its face, it would be superfluous to do so.

Myth #7—Israeli military action against its neighbors is only taken to defend itself against terrorism.

The facts tell another story. Take, for instance, the devastating 1982 Israeli war on Lebanon. As political analyst Noam Chomsky extensively documents in his epic analysis "The Fateful Triangle," this military offensive was carried out with barely even the thinnest veil of a pretext.

While one may read contemporary accounts insisting this war was fought in response to a constant shelling of northern Israeli by the PLO, then based in Lebanon, the truth is that, despite continuous Israeli provocations, the PLO had with only a few exceptions abided by a cease-fire that had been in place. Moreover, in each of those instances, it was Israel that had first violated the cease-fire.

Among the Israeli provocations, throughout early 1982, it attacked and sank Lebanese fishing boats and otherwise committed hundreds of violations of Lebanese territorial waters. It committed thousands of violations of Lebanese airspace, yet never did manage to provoke the PLO response it sought to serve as the casus belli for the planned invasion of Lebanon.

On May 9, Israel bombed Lebanon, an act that was finally met with a PLO response when it launched rocket and artillery fire into Israel.

Then a terrorist group headed by Abu Nidal attempted to assassinate Israeli Ambassador Shlomo Argov in London. Although the PLO itself had been at war with Abu Nidal, who had been condemned to death by a Fatah military tribunal in 1973, and despite the fact that Abu Nidal was not based in Lebanon, Israel cited this event as a pretext to bomb the Sabra and Shatila refugee camps, killing 200 Palestinians. The PLO responded by shelling settlements in northern Israel. Yet Israel did not manage to provoke the kind of larger-scale response it was looking to use as a casus belli for its planned invasion.

As Israeli scholar Yehoshua Porath has suggested, Israel's decision to invade Lebanon, far from being a response to PLO attacks, rather "flowed from the very fact that the cease-fire had been observed." Writing in the Israeli daily Haaretz, Porath assessed that "The government's hope is that the stricken PLO, lacking a logistic and territorial base, will return to its earlier terrorism.... In this way, the PLO will lose part of the political legitimacy that it has gained … undercutting the danger that elements will develop among the Palestinians that might become a legitimate negotiating partner for future political accommodations."

As another example, take Israel's Operation Cast Lead from December 27, 2008 to January 18, 2009. Prior to Israel's assault on the besieged and defenseless population of the Gaza Strip, Israel had entered into a cease-fire agreement with the governing authority there, Hamas. Contrary to popular myth, it was Israel, not Hamas, who ended the cease-fire.

The pretext for Operation Cast Lead is obligatorily described in Western media accounts as being the "thousands" of rockets that Hamas had been firing into Israel prior to the offensive, in violation of the cease-fire.

The truth is that from the start of the cease-fire in June until November 4, Hamas fired no rockets, despite numerous provocations from Israel, including stepped-up operations in the West Bank and Israeli soldiers taking pop-shots at Gazans across the border, resulting in several injuries and at least one death.

On November 4, it was again Israel who violated the cease-fire, with airstrikes and a ground invasion of Gaza that resulted in further deaths. Hamas finally responded with rocket fire, and from that point on the cease-fire was effectively over, with daily tit-for-tat attacks from both sides.

Despite Israel's lack of good faith, Hamas offered to renew the cease-fire from the time it was set to officially expire in December. Israel rejected the offer, preferring instead to inflict violent collective punishment on the people of Gaza.

As the Israeli Intelligence and Terrorism Information Center noted, the truce "brought relative quiet to the western Negev population," with 329 rocket and mortar attacks, "most of them during the month and a half after November 4," when Israel had violated and effectively ended the truce. This stands in remarkable contrast to the 2,278 rocket and mortar attacks in the six months prior to the truce. Until November 4, the center also observed, "Hamas was careful to maintain the ceasefire."

If Israel had desired to continue to mitigate the threat of Palestinian militant rocket attacks, it would have simply not ended the cease-fire, which was very highly effective in reducing the number of such attacks, including eliminating all such attacks by Hamas. It would not have instead resorted to violence, predictably resulting in a greatly escalated threat of retaliatory rocket and mortar attacks from Palestinian militant groups.

Moreover, even if Israel could claim that peaceful means had been exhausted and that a resort military force to act in self-defense to defend its civilian population was necessary, that is demonstrably not what occurred. Instead, Israel deliberately targeted the civilian population of Gaza with systematic and deliberate disproportionate and indiscriminate attacks on residential areas, hospitals, schools, and other locations with protected civilian status under international law.

As the respected international jurist who headed up the United Nations investigation into the assault, Richard Goldstone, has observed, the means by which Israel carried out Operation Cast Lead were not consistent with its stated aims, but was rather more indicative of a deliberate act of collective punishment of the civilian population.

Myth #8—God gave the land to the Jews, so the Arabs are the occupiers.

No amount of discussion of the facts on the ground will ever convince many Jews and Christians that Israel could ever do wrong, because they view its actions as having the hand of God behind it, and that its policies are in fact the will of God. They believe that God gave the land of Palestine, including the West Bank and Gaza Strip, to the Jewish people, and therefore Israel has a "right" to take it by force from the Palestinians, who, in this view, are the wrongful occupiers of the land.

But one may simply turn to the pages of their own holy books to demonstrate the fallaciousness of this or similar beliefs. Christian Zionists are fond of quoting passages from the Bible such as the following to support their Zionist beliefs:

"And Yahweh said to Abram, after Lot had separated from him: 'Lift your eyes now and look from the place where you are – northward, southward, eastward, and westward; for all the land which you see I give to you and your descendants forever. And I will make your descendants as the dust of the earth; so that if a man could number the dust of the earth, then your descendants could also be numbered. Arise, walk in the land through its length and its width, for I give it to you." (Genesis 13:14-17)

"Then Yahweh appeared to him and said: 'Do not go down to Egypt; live in the land of which I shall tell you. Dwell in the land, and I will be with you and bless you; for to you and your descendants I give all these lands, and I will perform the oath which I swore to Abraham your father." (Genesis 26: 1-3)

"And behold, Yahweh stood above it and said: 'I am Yahweh, God of Abraham your father, and the God of Isaac; the land on which you lie I will give to you and your descendants." (Genesis 28:13)

Yet Christian Zionists conveniently disregard other passages providing further context for understanding this covenant, such as the following:

"You shall therefore keep all My statutes and all My judgments, and perform them, that the land where I am bringing you to dwell may not vomit you out." (Leviticus 20:22)

"But if you do not obey Me, and do not observe all these commandments ... but break My covenant ... I will bring the land to desolation, and your enemies who dwell in it shall be astonished at it. I will scatter you among the nations and draw out a sword after you; your land shall be desolate and your cities waste ... You shall perish among the nations, and the land of your enemies shall eat you up." (Leviticus 26: 14, 15, 32-33, 28)

"Therefore Yahweh was very angry with Israel, and removed them from His sight; there was none left but the tribe of Judah alone.... So Israel was carried away from their own land to Assyria, as it is to this day." (2 Kings 17:18, 23)

"And I said, after [Israel] had done all these things, 'Return to Me.' But she did not return. And her treacherous sister Judah saw it. Then I saw that for all the causes for which backsliding Israel had committed adultery, I had put her away and given her a certificate of divorce; yet her treacherous sister Judah did not fear, but went and played the harlot also." (Jeremiah 3: 7-8)

Yes, in the Bible, Yahweh, the God of Abraham, Isaac, and Israel, told the Hebrews that the land could be theirs—if they would obey his commandments. Yet, as the Bible tells the story, the Hebrews were rebellious against Yahweh in all their generations.

What Jewish and Christian Zionists omit from their Biblical arguments in favor of continued Israel occupation is that Yahweh also told the Hebrews, including the tribe of Judah (from whom the "Jews" are descended), that he would remove them from the land if they broke the covenant by rebelling against his commandments, which is precisely what occurs in the Bible.

Thus, the theological argument for Zionism is not only bunk from a secular point of view, but is also a wholesale fabrication from a scriptural perspective, representing a continued rebelliousness against Yahweh and his Torah, and the teachings of Yeshua the Messiah (Jesus the Christ) in the New Testament.

Myth #9—Palestinians reject the two-state solution because they want to destroy Israel.

In an enormous concession to Israel, Palestinians have long accepted the two-state solution. The elected representatives of the Palestinian people in Yasser Arafat's Palestine Liberation Organization (PLO) had since the 70s recognized the state of Israel and accepted the two-state solution to the conflict. Despite this, Western media continued through the 90s to report that the PLO rejected this solution and instead wanted to wipe Israel off the map.

The pattern has been repeated since Hamas was voted into power in the 2006 Palestinian elections. Although Hamas has for years accepted the reality of the state of Israel and demonstrated a willingness to accept a Palestinian state in the West Bank and Gaza Strip alongside Israel, it is virtually obligatory for Western mainstream media, even today, to report that Hamas rejects the two-state solution, that it instead seeks "to destroy Israel."

In fact, in early 2004, shortly before he was assassinated by Israel, Hamas founder Sheik Ahmed Yassin said that Hamas could accept a Palestinian state alongside Israel. Hamas has since repeatedly reiterated its willingness to accept a two-state solution.

In early 2005, Hamas issued a document stating its goal of seeking a Palestinian state alongside Israel and recognizing the 1967 borders.

The exiled head of the political bureau of Hamas, Khalid Mish'al, wrote in the London Guardian in January 2006 that Hamas was "ready to make a just peace." He wrote that "We shall never recognize the right of any power to rob us of our land and deny us our national rights.... But if you are willing to accept the principle of a long-term truce, we are prepared to negotiate the terms."

During the campaigning for the 2006 elections, the top Hamas official in Gaza, Mahmoud al-Zahar said that Hamas was ready to "accept to establish our independent state on the area occupied [in] '67," a tacit recognition of the state of Israel.

The elected prime minister from Hamas, Ismail Haniyeh, said in February 2006 that Hamas accepted "the establishment of a Palestinian state" within the "1967 borders."

In April 2008, former U.S. President Jimmy Carter met with Hamas officials and afterward stated that Hamas "would accept a Palestinian state on the 1967 borders" and would "accept the right of Israel to live as a neighbor next door in peace." It was Hamas' "ultimate goal to see Israel living in their allocated borders, the 1967 borders, and a contiguous, vital Palestinian state alongside."

That same month Hamas leader Meshal said, "We have offered a truce if Israel withdraws to the 1967 borders, a truce of 10 years as a proof of recognition."

In 2009, Meshal said that Hamas "has accepted a Palestinian state on the 1967 borders."

Hamas' shift in policy away from total rejection of the existence of the state of Israel towards acceptance of the international consensus on a two-state solution to the conflict is in no small part a reflection of the will of the Palestinian public. A public opinion survey from April of last year, for instance, found that three out of four Palestinians were willing to accept a two-state solution.

Myth #10—The U.S. is an honest broker and has sought to bring about peace in the Middle East.

Rhetoric aside, the U.S. supports Israel's policies, including its illegal occupation and other violations of international humanitarian law. It supports Israel's criminal policies financially, militarily, and diplomatically.

The Obama administration, for example, stated publically that it was opposed to Israel's settlement policy and ostensibly "pressured" Israel to freeze colonization activities. Yet very early on, the administration announced that it would not cut back financial or military aid to Israel, even if it defied international law and continued settlement construction. That message was perfectly well understood by the Netanyahu government in Israel, which continued its colonization policies.

To cite another straightforward example, both the U.S. House of Representatives and the Senate passed resolutions openly declaring support for Israel's Operation Cast Lead, despite a constant stream of reports evidencing Israeli war crimes.

On the day the U.S. Senate passed its resolution "reaffirming the United States' strong support for Israel in its battle with Hamas" (January 8, 2009), the International Committee of the Red Cross (ICRC) issued a statement demanding that Israel allow it to assist victims of the conflict because the Israeli military had blocked access to wounded Palestinians—a war crime under international law.

That same day, U.N. Secretary General Ban Ki-moon issued a statement condemning Israel for firing on a U.N. aid convoy delivering humanitarian supplies to Gaza and for the killing of two U.N. staff members—both further war crimes.

On the day that the House passed its own version of the resolution, the U.N. announced that it had had to stop humanitarian work in Gaza because of numerous incidents in which its staff, convoys, and installations, including clinics and schools, had come under Israeli attack.

U.S. financial support for Israel surpasses $3 billion annually. When Israel waged a war to punish the defenseless civilian population of Gaza, its pilots flew U.S.-made F-16 fighter-bombers and Apache helicopter gunships, dropping U.S.-made bombs, including the use of white phosphorus munitions in violation of international law.

U.S. diplomatic support for Israeli crimes includes its use of the veto power in the U.N. Security Council. When Israel was waging a devastating war against the civilian population and infrastructure of Lebanon in the summer of 2006, the U.S. vetoed a cease-fire resolution.

As Israel was waging Operation Cast Lead, the U.S. delayed the passage of a resolution calling for an end to the violence, and then abstained rather than criticize Israel once it finally allowed the resolution to be put to a vote.

When the U.N. Human Rights Council officially adopted the findings and recommendations of its investigation into war crimes during Operation Cast Lead, headed up by Richard Goldstone, the U.S. responded by announcing its intention to block any effort to have the Security Council similarly adopt its conclusions and recommendations. The U.S. Congress passed a resolution rejecting the Goldstone report because it found that Israel had committed war crimes.

Through its virtually unconditional support for Israel, the U.S. has effectively blocked any steps to implement the two-state solution to the Israeli-Palestinian conflict. The so-called "peace process" has for many decades consisted of U.S. and Israeli rejection Palestinian self-determination and blocking of any viable Palestinian state.

> "Given the long history of the Arab-
> Israeli conflict and failure of the
> many attempts at negotiations, I
> have come to the reluctant conclusion
> that both sides cannot come to an
> agreement by themselves."

The International Community Must Look Past the Flawed Narratives Perpetuated by Each Side

Sylvain Ehrenfeld

In the following viewpoint Sylvain Ehrenfeld states his belief that both sides of this particular Middle East battle must compromise and understand the issues facing their so-called enemy. He believes that Hamas and the Palestinian Authority must accept the right of Israel to exist and that Israel must ease the hardships it has inflicted upon the Palestinian people. The author feels that only through such recognition and a willingness to come together can peace be achieved in the region. Ehrenfeld is a member of the Ethical Culture Society of Bergen County in New Jersey, which focuses on ethics and human flourishing as keys to strengthening society.

As you read, consider the following questions:

1. Does the author take one side or the other in the debate about the righteousness of the Gaza blockade?
2. What point does the author make about the importance of accepting Israel's right to exist?
3. Does the author come across as optimistic about a negotiated settlement?

Because this is a very difficult and emotional subject, I think it's helpful for you to know something about my background. It is, at least in part, a basis for my point of view. I grew up in Antwerp, Belgium, and lived there until the age of 11. I came to New York in 1940 in what I think was the last boat before Germany invaded. The reason I'm alive and here is because of my mother. She was organizing a soup kitchen feeding refugees from Germany, and she heard the stories and convinced my father to leave. I was aware of anti-Semitism from my early years.

As a young academic, I spent three years helping to develop a Department of Industrial Engineering at the Technion in Haifa, Israel on a project supported by the Israeli and America governments.

Each side in the Israeli-Palestinian conflict has its own narrative telling some of the truth. What is important for understanding of both sides is to know what they leave out. Each side interprets events in terms of their own story, demonizes the other and omits their own contribution to the conflict. Each side is in a state of denial, ignoring the response to their own actions.

The Palestinian story focuses on victimhood, their suffering and dispossession and their deep sense of injustice at being punished because of Europe's treatment of Jews. They leave out the history of initiating wars, their violence, their faulty leadership and their constant refusal to take opportunities for accommodation.

The Israeli story emphasizes their long-time historic attachment to the land, the legitimacy granted by the UN partition plan, the hostility and constant threat of wars coming from their neighbors, and the rejection of their peace offers. Underlying it all is the ever-present trauma of the holocaust. They leave out their own role. They rationalize and downgrade the cruelties of the occupation. They further aggravate the situation by the historic western attitude of both condescending to and mostly disregarding the local Palestinian population.

In order to have some insight into past, present and possible future, we need some history and background. Then we return to the importance of narratives.

A first question—why choose that particular corner of the Middle East as a haven for the Jewish people? Given the long attachment of Judaism to the Holy Land, and the disastrous history of Jewish suffering in Europe, the Jews needed to have a place to go where they would be accepted as Jews. Where would they have gone after World War 2? Chaim Weizmann, the first President of Israel said, "the world seemed to be divided into parts—those places where Jews could not live and those where they could not enter."

At present Jews are the majority in Israel. 5.5 million citizens of Israel are Jews and 1.3 million are Arabs. Arabs compose 20% of the Israeli population. They are second class citizens suffering a great deal of discrimination. Most Israelis would not deny this, while allowing for the fact that there are Arabs in the Knesset. The press in Israel is among the freest in the world, and most certainly in the Middle East. The Israeli judiciary is really independent. Still, the large numbers of Arab citizens may become a problem. They have recently become more vocal.

I am concerned about the current situation in Israel and the situation of the Palestinians. It is at a political and military impasse that is becoming increasingly dangerous. Given the attacks by Hezbollah from Lebanon, and the steady influx of a complicated mix of weapons that are becoming ever more sophisticated and far reaching, given the fact that these weapons are used by a guerrilla army that mingles with the general population, Israel's military strength is less effective. Hezbollah is generously supported by

Iran. Armed Israeli response only increases the anger of Arab populations all over the world.

In my opinion this anger has long been very convenient for autocratic Arab governments, serving as a distraction from the poverty, frustration and powerlessness of what commentators call the "Arab street." In my view, it is both to Israel's benefit, and an urgent need, to settle the bitter relationship with the Palestinians. The consequences of not doing so are too serious.

Why hasn't this conflict been settled for the past 100 years? The history of Israel has always been intertwined with the UN. The partition plan of 1947 was the source for the creation of the State of Israel by the UN. The Arabs revolted against partition, a civil war began, the Arab governments joined the war, and the borders were decided by an armistice in 1949.

The struggle between the State of Israel and the Arabs living within the area has always come before world attention within the context of the UN. We need to know this background to see what is possible and where we go from here. When Ben Gurion came to Palestine in 1906, there were about 700,000 inhabitants, of whom 55,000 were Jews. Only about 550 could be defined as Zionist pioneers. The Jewish population was 8%. Demographically, Palestine was overwhelmingly Arab. In a British census of 1922, the percentage of Jews rose to something like 11%. By 1947 it had risen to 33%. Jerusalem was always mostly Jewish.

Israel Zangwill, a writer and early Zionist, said, "Israel was a land without people, for a people without land." This was clearly not the case. Not all Zionists saw it this way. Asher Ginzberg, better known by his literary name, Ahad Ha'am (One of the People) was a distinguished cultural Zionist. As early as the 1890's he called attention to the presence of the Arabs on the land. He said the relationship would be difficult and enduring. The problem wouldnt go away.

The Arabs saw an increasing number of Jews coming to what they saw as their land—buying up property and becoming more organized—a serious threat that made them feel increasingly dispossessed. Many Jews preferred to ignore the signs, until riots broke out in 1921 and 1929. They attacked Jewish neighborhoods. The Arabs call it a popular uprising, not riots. Some observers began to view the problem as two groups competing for the same land and population dominance.

Chaim Weizmann, First President of Israel, saw the difficulty of the problem in tragic terms, as a conflict between two rights. Even Ben Gurion, at times, acknowledged that the Arabs had legitimate rights. For example, Ben Gurion to the Jewish agency in 1936: "I want you to see things—with Arab eyes—they see immigration on a large scale. They see lands passing into our hands. They see England identifying with Zionism." So did Jabotinsky, the founder of the Herut movement, who was more outspoken. What he said was, "It's them or us." Then came the British Mandate, the Balfour Declaration, giving the Jews a national home, and expanding Zionism. In the late 30's the feelings of the Arabs boiled over in a revolt which was ruthlessly suppressed by the British, aided by some Jews and some wealthy Arabs. To placate the Arabs, Britain restricted Jewish immigration. This was, of course, strongly opposed by Jewish groups.

Britain organized the Peel Commission to report on this difficult situation. In 1937 the Commission reported: "there is an irrepressible conflict between two national communities within the narrow bounds of one small country ... there is no common ground between them." The report recommended partition. During World War 2 the Grand Mufti of Jerusalem, who was vehemently anti-Semitic, sided with the Nazis. The Jews formed a brigade and fought with the Allies. This brigade was at first opposed by the British who were suspicious of their postwar goals.

After the war the UN organized a commission to study the situation and came to the same conclusion as the Peel Commission. A partition plan won UN approval. Ben Gurion then declared the State of Israel. The Arabs did not accept the plan, and war broke out. The war took place in two phases, firstly a civil war between Jews and Arabs in Israel. As civil wars are, it was fierce and cruel with many deaths. Then, in the second phase, the neighboring Arabs invaded. The war ended in 1949 with an armistice.

In response to the situation, the UN passed the first of many resolutions—194, relating to the right of return of refugees. This constituted about 700,000 Arabs. For several reasons the Israeli state did not accept this resolution. Firstly, accepting so many people of a hostile population would constitute a fifth column. Secondly they pointed out that an equal number of Jews were expelled from Arab countries. Finally, after the end of World War 2, massive immigration of Jews was taking place. After expulsion from both Europe and North Africa, these immigrants were finding a home in Israel. They had no other place to go.

After much discussion and pressure, the Israeli government offered to accept 100,000 Arab refugees. But the whole question became moot for an ironic reason. The Arabs rejected the offer of the return of 100,000 refugees, and all rejected Resolution 194, because they viewed it as a recognition of Israel's right to exist. From their point of view there was no sharing and no compromise— Jews had no place in Palestine. The refugees and many of their descendants have remained in camps all these years, leading a dislocated life, surviving on UN assistance, virtually ignored by the Arab governments.

In Israel there is much debate as to why and how these refugees were displaced. Benny Morris, the Israeli historian, has studied these brutal times in great detail. Some fled from warfare, some were forcibly kicked out, some were urged by Arab armies to flee with the promise that they could return after victory. How many were kicked out is in contention by Israeli historians. One observation about the partition plan—you have only to look at a map to see how impossible it was for any kind of coexistence. Each state was not a solid block of population. Instead there were little mixed pockets of population. The map was drawn simply to follow the demography. It made no provision for ethnic or political considerations. Two peoples who had been locked in a bitter fight for decades were thrown together.

Did the Arab governments help from a humanitarian point of view? Not particularly. The Palestinians have remained unpopular in large parts of the Arab world. When Egypt was in control of Gaza, from 1949 into 1967, Gaza Arabs were rarely allowed to travel into Egypt. After the first Gulf war in 1991, Kuwait expelled 250,000 Palestinians. Only Jordan allows Palestinians to become citizens. Elsewhere in the Arab world they are not permitted to become citizens. Even in Jordan, war broke out, suppressed by the Jordanian government. The Palestinian-Israeli conflict has been a superbly effective scapegoat and distraction for the Arab masses, who rank very poorly in the UN's human development index in relation to the rest of the world.

The Six-Day War in 1967 created a fundamental change for Israel. Because Israel conquered the territories of the West Bank and Gaza, these lands with their millions of Palestinians came under Israeli occupation. Then followed the much discussed Resolution 242. The UN stipulated that Israel should withdraw essentially to the 1967 borders, as part of an overall agreement and a recognition of Israel's right to live in peace and security. The resolution acknowledges the Arab's rights to these lands, and Israel's right to peace and security. Israel expected to trade land for peace. In June 1967, Moshe Dayan said, "We are waiting for the Arabs' phone call. They know where to find us." The answer was given in Khartoum on September, 1967.

The major Arab states rejected the principles of Resolution 242, and announced their policy towards Israel—the three Nos: No recognition, no peace, no negotiations. Israel became the occupier of an angry and unhappy population. Living under occupation is terrible for the occupied. It is not a blessing for the occupier.

Arthur Herzberg, former Rabbi in Englewood, and former President of the American Jewish Congress, tells a remarkable story in his book, The Fate of Zionism. After Israel's victory, there was great jubilation. David Ben Gurion, former Prime Minister, had left politics and moved to a kibbutz in the Negev. He was invited to speak at a Labor Party meeting and arrived late, in traditional kibbutznik style, in shorts. He astounded everyone by saying that if Israel did not immediately return all the territory it had just captured, with the exception of East Jerusalem, it would be heading for a historic disaster.

Given the consequence all these years later, the loss of Israeli lives, the increasing demonization of Israel in the Arab press and in some parts of the world press, and to some degree in world opinion, in addition to the intifadas, the great suffering and humiliation of the Palestinians, the damage to the lives of both sides, it is becoming increasingly clear that Ben Gurion was right. He had the foresight to see that time passing only made it more difficult for Israel to protect its citizens and maintain control over a huge angry population. This is a cycle of violence and despair.

For Israel the situation is a trap. Israel cannot stay without creeping annexation that includes more Arabs into Israeli society— the demographic issue—or leave, certainly not easily with all its many settlers. Also, what happens to the millions of Palestinians in the West Bank? Can they become citizens of Israel?

Now, in Israel there is much discussion of the demographic dilemma. Only about 50% of the people living between the Jordan River and the Mediterranean are Jews. By the year 2020, the percentage of Jews will be 42%.

Currently, Israeli Prime Minister Ehud Olmert has been heavily criticized for the conduct of the war with Hezbollah. To shore up his faltering government he turned sharply to the right and chose a hard liner, Avigdor Lieberman, for the cabinet. Lieberman is known for his extremely hawkish views. At one time he called for stripping Israeli Arabs of citizenship. This kind of talk makes an impossible situation even more impossible, if that is possible.

A two state solution seems like the way to go. The most detailed attempt was pursued by President Clinton, bringing together Israeli Prime Minister Barak, and Yasser Arafat. The first map outlining borders proposed by Israel has often been cited by the Palestinians as a ridiculous offer—a Bantustan plan of non-contiguous cantons, giving the Palestinians nothing that could be called a state. People have been left with the impression that this was the Israeli position. The final map, reflecting Clinton's final proposal to which Barak agreed, was a contiguous area, encompassing most of the West Bank. It was the most reasonable deal to date, but it was rejected by Arafat. There were some weaknesses in the deal—for example—ambiguity over control of the air space over the projected Palestinian state. The real weakness was that the Barak coalition had unravelled and he was now in a minority in the Knesset. However, even if the plan had not been approved by the Knesset, it could have become a signpost for a projected peace and a basis of hopes for the future, the signalling of a willingness to seriously negotiate the peace that both sides really need. Arafat rejected the plan and made no counter-offer. Sharon was elected, and the intifada broke out.

Clinton stated that the plan broke down essentially about the right of return of the refugees. Arafat told Clinton that if he accepted, Clinton could attend his funeral. Perhaps what is most important for the understanding of the conflict is that the plan clearly calls for a final resolution and an end to any further claims. This is the psychological sticking point for the Palestinians. They are interested in their concept of peace and justice—a vindication of their grievance. Unlike Israelis who are very tough negotiators, but also pragmatic and interested in solutions. Palestinians and Arab leaders take no responsibility for the disaster they have brought on their own people, both by the ineptness of their leadership and the autocracy and corruption of their governments.

Abba Eban was once quoted as saying, "Palestinian leadership never misses an opportunity to miss an opportunity for peace."

The election of Hamas was in part a reproach to the corruption of the Palestinian National Authority and in part because of the political ineptness of the Abbas party who ran too many candidates against a well-organized religious fundamentalist party with only a few candidates. Hamas, in spite of its charitable record, since they are responsible for much of the social services Palestinians get, still did not win a majority in the popular vote. However, both Hamas in the West Bank and Gaza, and Hezbollah in Lebanon, are ideologically and religiously opposed to any kind of agreement on a political solution. They believe that Palestine, as stated in their charter, belongs entirely to Moslems. To relinquish any part of the land is forbidden. (Some Orthodox Jews have a similar belief. God promised this land to the Jews and no one can give it up.)

Yet it has become clear that a military solution is impossible. Even worse—ongoing conflict is becoming ever more dangerous. If the nature of the conflict moves from the secular to the religious, we can only expect more bloodletting since it is against God's will to compromise.

At present given this history the worst aspect of the problem is that both Palestinians and the leadership of some of the Arab/Moslem states have refused to accept the legitimacy of Israel and realistic negotiations about the right of return of refugees to villages which no longer exist. Whatever the average Israeli and Palestinian thinks about a two-state solution, the constant violence supported and maintained by arms shipments allows extremists to sabotage any deal, even as it begins to take place.

Given the long history of the Arab-Israeli conflict and failure of the many attempts at negotiations, I have come to the reluctant conclusion that both sides cannot come to an agreement by themselves. Arthur Herzberg and Shlomo Ben-Ami, former Foreign Minister of Israel and key participant in the Camp David talks, have come to the same conclusion. There is no military solution. Neither side can impose its will on the other. All further hostilities will only inflict more cruelty on both peoples. Israel's safety has been thought to depend on deterrence, the idea that any attack can be handled by overwhelming force. The Lebanese conflict with Hezbollah's effectiveness in fighting Israel has put the deterrence doctrine in question, making the situation much more dangerous.

A political solution must be found, and can only happen with concerted international action. The US, which at one time had the credibility to appear as an honest broker, has lost this power since its entanglement in Iraq. The need for participation by the Arab League is absolutely necessary. Once, in 2002, they proposed a vague initiative. As the situation becomes more and more threatening and dangerous, because of the availability of sophisticated long distance weapons, they may become more willing to participate in negotiations. In fact, they have recently shown renewed interest. Growing Shiite radicalism threatens the Sunni governments. Rage against Israel can rebound against these same governments. Unsettling wars in this area could create economic havoc. From the Israeli point of view, the acknowledgement of the limits of military power could influence Israel if there was a real chance of an agreement.

The outlines of a reasonable agreement are fairly clear from the implementation of Resolution 242 and the Clinton parameters of 2000. Is pressure likely to be more effective now? In the recent hostilities between Israel and Hezbollah in Lebanon, the US was at first reluctant to demand an immediate ceasefire to give Israel time to control Hezbollah. When the situation looked as if it might spiral out of control, the major powers in the Security Council were able to act decisively and effectively to bring peacekeepers into the area. This demonstrates how the major powers in the Security Council can impose solutions if they choose. They may decide to do so in the Arab-Israeli conflict if they think the situation in the region is becoming too unstable and too dangerous. There is some good reason for this. The weapons involved are becoming more and more sophisticated, with potential to ignite a regional war and create chaos. One proposal is to put UN peacekeepers in the West Bank.

Finally, returning to the idea of narratives—Sami Adwan, a Palestinian educator, met with Dan Bar-On, an Israeli social psychologist. They have worked together since 2002 developing three booklets called Learning The Other's Narrative, to be used in Palestinian and Israeli high schools. Each side is confronted with a contradictory version of history. Each page is divided into three: the Palestinian and Israeli narratives, and a third section left blank for the pupil to fill in. The purpose is not to legitimize or accept the other's narrative, but to recognize it. The booklets have been translated into English, Spanish, Italian, Catalan and Basque, and will soon appear in German. In France it has sold more than 23,000 copies. It has also been adapted for use for the Macedonian-Albanian narratives.

There have been great difficulties in introducing the booklets into Palestinian and Israeli high schools. However, more and more people in these communities are urging a change in the teaching of history. Understanding the other's narrative is essential for progress, and as well, essential for humanist thinking and ethical action.

> "*After not having to tone down his anti-Israel rhetoric during the eight years of the pro-Palestinian Obama administration, Abbas is evidently feeling pressure to change his anti-Semitic tone with the pro-Israel Trump administration.*"

Israel Is Simply Protecting Its Right to Exist

Michael F. Haverluck

In the following viewpoint Michael F. Haverluck argues that Israel has every right to use all available means to protect itself against Hamas, which he states has made no secret of its intent to wipe the Jewish state off the world map. The author also condemns those he feels have been led to believe that the Palestinians are willing to work with Israel toward a peaceful solution that would guarantee Israeli sovereignty. Haverluck writes for American Family News Network.

"Palestinian Factions Reject Israel's Right to Exist," by Michael F. Haverluck, American Family News Network (OneNewsNow.com), April 30, 2017. Reprinted by permission.

As you read, consider the following questions:

1. How does conservatism in general align with the belief that Israel has the right to maintain a blockade of Gaza?
2. Does the author touch upon the humanitarian issues involved in the blockade?
3. What is the author's main argument?

Last month, leaders of Fatah announced on official Palestinian Authority TV that their jihadist organization and Hamas— which have been competing for political power and discussing the formation of a unity government for years—agree that Israel has no right to exist, stressing that they refuse to recognize the State of Israel.

"The Fatah Movement never demanded that Hamas recognize Israel," Fatah Central Committee member and Commissioner of Treasury and Economy Muhammad Shtayyeh told Palestinian Media Watch (PMW) on its Topic of the Day on March 26. "To this moment, Fatah does not recognize Israel. The topic of recognition of Israel has not been raised in any of Fatah's conferences."

Competing Factions Unified on Anti-Israel Stance

Hamas leadership also believes that Israel must be wiped off the face of the map and make room for a Palestinian takeover.

Mahmoud Al-Zahar, who serves as a member of the Hamas movement's political bureau, declared that his group's new charter to establish a Palestinian state in the West Bank and the Gaza Strip is just one strategic move in its ultimate plan predicated on Hamas's openly admitted belief that all of Israel is actually "Palestine."

"Our principles say that our land is all of Palestine—including the land that is under occupation [i.e., Israel]," Al-Zahar proclaimed on the Lebanese television channel Al-Mayadeen. "[Establishing a state in the West Bank and Gaza] is a tactical step that does not harm the right of the Palestinians to all of the land of Palestine."

The Islamic faction leader went on to stress that not all the Jewish people are the Hamas movement's enemies—just the ones who occupy "Palestine."

"We are not a copy of Fatah," Al-Zahar emphasized, according to PMW. "We are not a copy of a failed project."

PA Maneuvering for American Support

Even though Abbas is not shy about sharing Hamas' and Fatah's hatred for Israel, the Muslim leader has shown signs of loosening the P.A.'s ties with Hamas in order to gain favor with Trump.

"Palestinian Authority President Mahmoud Abbas may be trying to distance his Ramallah-based government from the Hamas-ruled Gaza Strip by cutting off funding for electricity to Gaza," CBN News reported. "But the two groups still hold their hatred for Israel in common."

After not having to tone down his anti-Israel rhetoric during the eight years of the pro-Palestinian Obama administration, Abbas is evidently feeling pressure to change his anti-Semitic tone with the pro-Israel Trump administration.

"Trump is arguably the most pro-Israel president in the White House for years," CBN News' Tzippe Barrow noted. "That may be making Abbas a little jittery."

While politicians have been propagating the idea of a peaceful Palestinian state coexisting alongside Israel for decades, Zionist Organization of America National President Morton Klein argues that the facts indicate that negotiations for a durable settlement with Israel are nothing more than a belabored myth.

"The idea that the Palestinian Arab leadership and society accept Israel and desire a durable peace settlement with the Jewish State is one of the most persistent myths that one hears repeated endlessly," Klein insisted, according to CBN News.

However, in an apparent attempt to convince the United States that the P.A. is taking measures to work with Israel, officials of the Arab government informed the Jewish State that it will cut off its funding of Gaza's power.

"Ahead of the meeting in Washington, P.A. officials told Israel Defense Forces (IDF) Coordinator of Government Activities in the Territories (COGAT) Thursday it won't pay for electricity anymore that Israel supplies to Gaza," Barrow informed. "Hamas shuts down Gaza's sole power plant from time to time ostensibly due to fuel shortages—rationing electricity to residents to as little as four hours a day."

Yet Gaza's electricity crunch is nothing new, as Hamas has done little over the past decade to stabilize the flow of electricity —much of which is supplied from outside its territory.

"Israel provides 125 megawatts of electricity to Gaza—about 30 percent of its daily needs through 10 power lines," Barrow pointed out. "Egypt provides 27 megawatts—plus another 60-80 megawatts—through a power station that's also been offline due to lack of fuel. Since Hamas took control of Gaza in June 2007, power outages are by no means a new phenomenon."

Abbas: World Must Recognize "Palestine" as a State

Despite the fact that two competing factions within the territory governed by the P.A. refuse to recognize the State of Israel, Abbas has consistently demanded that the United Nations (UN) force the recognition of Palestine as a State. He recently told the global "peacekeeping" agency that the best way to preserve the two-state solution and end the Israeli-Palestinian conflict is for all nations to agree that Israel must surrender its land to the Palestinians.

"We call on countries that have recognized Israel and believe in the two-state solution to defend and support this solution by recognizing the State of Palestine," Abbas declared on February 27 while giving his address to the 34th session of the UN Human Rights Council in Geneva, according to the Jerusalem Post.

He petitioned the council to force a unilateral acknowledgement of a Palestinian state as an act of championing so-called "human rights."

"Palestine will remain the greatest test for this council, and its success in defending human rights in Palestine will determine the sustainability of human rights across the world," Abbas orated as the first of 107 international dignitaries to address the council on the first day of the month-long session. "We must not fail this test."

Israeli Ambassador to the UN in New York, Danny Danon, condemned the global agency for continuing its anti-Israel agenda by hosting Abbas and highlighting his speech above all others to open the session.

"It is no surprise that this council—which has long been divorced from reality—has chosen once again to provide a platform for Palestinian smears against us," Dannon contended, as reported by the Post. "It is time that Abbas and the Palestinian leadership understand that a new era has dawned at the UN in which speeches and one-sided initiatives against Israel will not succeed. The only way forward is through direct negotiations with Israel."

> "*The Palestinian leadership baulks at supporting a Jewish state. This intransigence has repeatedly stood in the way of statehood and weakened the Palestinian position.*"

Israel Will Never Cede Its Right to Exist

Nyunggai Warren Mundine

In the following viewpoint Nyunggai Warren Mundine argues that the Israeli-Palestinian conflict will never end if the Palestinian Authority does not recognize Israel's right to exist. The author wrote this viewpoint after a rare visit to his country by Israeli leader Benjamin Netanyahu. He makes clear that he sympathizes with the historic plight of Israel and understands the hardline stance taken by its government against those he believes must ensure its right to exist. Mundine feels that only through giving that assurance can the Palestinians ever realize their dream of securing a state of their own. Mundine is an Australian Aboriginal leader and former president of the Australian Labor Party.

"Jews Are the First Peoples of Israel—with a Right to Exist," by Nyunggai Warren Mundine, *Australian Financial Review*, March 6, 2017. Reprinted by permission.

As you read, consider the following questions:

1. How did the visit of Benjamin Netanyahu to Australia affect the views of the viewpoint author?
2. Does the author feel peace can be achieved without Palestinian recognition of Israel's sovereignty?
3. Should a historical perspective play any role in deciding the future of Israel and the Palestinian people?

Benjamin Netanyahu's visit to Australia was significant, both historically—the first visit by an Israeli Prime Minister—and for the future Australia-Israel relationship.

The relationship is founded on a strong base. Australia helped create Israel. In 1917 Australian soldiers helped defeat the Ottoman Empire's 400-year occupation of Palestine. Two days later Britain declared support for a Jewish national home there. In 1922 the League of Nations approved the Mandate for Palestine, appointing Britain mandatory power and tasking it with creating a Jewish state. This took 25 years, the UN adopting a partition plan for a Jewish state and an Arab state in 1947. Represented by former Labor leader "Doc" Evatt, Australia chaired the UN committee and cast the first General Assembly vote.

So I was disappointed that, during Netanyahu's visit, Labor luminaries Bob Hawke, Kevin Rudd and Gareth Evans called on Australia to formally recognise a Palestinian state. Symbolic recognition of a state when none exists is a hollow gesture that doesn't confront the elephant in the room: Palestinian leadership doesn't really support a two-state solution. Likewise, most Arab nations. They won't recognise Israel's right to exist.

The partition plan was a compromise in the face of Arab opposition to a Jewish state. Jews accepted the partition. Arabs didn't, wanting an Arab state only. Arab nations immediately invaded Israel. Israel won that war, gaining territory. Arab nations invaded Israel again unsuccessfully in 1967. Israel again gained territory, including East Jerusalem and the West Bank (from

Jordan) and Gaza and the Sinai Peninsula (from Egypt). Israel offered to return everything except East Jerusalem in exchange for recognition. Arab leaders refused, resolving instead to assist Arabs in those territories to resist Israel.

Withdrawal from Gaza

Since 1967 Israel has been under constant threat, surrounded by countries who would drive it off the face of the earth. It invaded South Lebanon in response to attacks, withdrawing in 2000 only to experience hundreds more terrorist attacks from that region.

In 1978 Israel returned Sinai to Egypt in exchange for peace. All Israeli settlements were removed and Egypt recognised the State of Israel.

In 2005 Israel unilaterally withdrew from Gaza, removing all settlements and handing control to the Palestinian Authority (PA). Gaza fell to Hamas who pursued its objective of destroying Israel. So Israel blockaded Gaza, allowing only humanitarian aid. Under Hamas, manufacturing and agriculture collapsed, unemployment rose to global highs and the economy fell into ruins. Gaza could have industry, trade and people commuting to Israel for work. Instead its people dig tunnels, plan suicide bombings and fire rockets.

Today the West Bank is administered in three areas. Area A, where most Palestinians live, has PA civil and security control. Area B has PA civil control and Israeli security control. Area C, where most Israeli settlements are, has Israeli civil and security control. Israelis and Palestinians live, work and do business together in and between Israel and the West Bank. But Israel restricts movement if required to manage security threats. These threats are encouraged by the PA who rewards Palestinians for attacking Israeli citizens with generous monthly payments. Last year, a Palestinian man killed a 13-year old Israeli girl in her bed. He was shot dead. Fatah (the PA's governing party) declared him a martyr. His mother called him a "hero." His family now receive monthly payments.

Sending the Wrong Signal

During Bill Clinton's presidency, Israel and the PA came within a hair's breadth of peace. Clinton blamed its failure on Palestinian leader Yasser Arafat. Clinton asked both parties to negotiate within set parameters on disputed issues or walk away. Israel agreed, offering Gaza and 97 per cent of the West Bank. Arafat refused. Clinton suggested Arafat "couldn't make the final jump from revolutionary to statesman." Arafat's actions support this. By always wearing military uniform, he sent the message he believed in military victory, not a peace pact.

Clinton said the main hold-outs were the right of return (allowing Palestinian refugees since 1948 and their descendants to move to Israel) and Israeli control of the Western Wall. Palestinian demands on these issues reflect a refusal to recognise a Jewish state. The Palestinian leadership believes the right of return will make Israel an Arab state by flooding it with Palestinians. Ceding Jewish claims to Jerusalem means acknowledging Jews' ancient and continuing presence there, contradicting Arab propaganda that Jews are interlopers in Israel, not its first peoples who lived there for millennia before Arab colonisation.

Sinai, Gaza and the West Bank demonstrate peace won't happen unless both sides agree and Israel's right to exist is respected.

The Palestinian leadership baulks at supporting a Jewish state. This intransigence has repeatedly stood in the way of statehood and weakened the Palestinian position. If not overcome, there will never be a Palestinian state. Israel has twice ceded settlements and land but will never cede its right to exist. Politicians shouldn't expect it to.

Periodical and Internet Sources Bibliography

The following articles have been selected to supplement the diverse views presented in this chapter.

BBC News. "Israel-Palestinian Conflict: Life in the Gaza Strip." BBC News, May 15, 2018. https://www.bbc.com/news/world-middle-east-20415675.

Zack Beauchamp. "11 Crucial Facts to Understand the Israel-Gaza Crisis." Vox, July 17, 2014. https://www.vox.com/2014/7/16/5904691/hamas-israel-gaza-11-things.

Jimmy Carter and Mary Robinson. "Gaza Blockade Must End." *Guardian*, August 5, 2014. https://www.theguardian.com/commentisfree/2014/aug/05/gaza-blockade-must-end-un-first-step-settlement.

Globe Staff. "What You Need to Know About the Gaza Border Violence and the Global Backlash Against Israel." *Globe and Mail*, May 18, 2018. https://www.theglobeandmail.com/world/article-what-you-need-to-know-about-the-recent-gaza-border-violence/.

Security Council. "Gaza Crisis Resulted from Collective Failure to Achieve Political Solution to Israeli-Palestinian Conflict, Security Council Told." United Nations, July 18, 2014. https://www.un.org/press/en/2014/sc11482.doc.htm.

Omar Shaban. "Consequences of the Israeli Blockade of Gaza." Fair Observer, July 25, 2014. https://www.fairobserver.com/region/middle_east_north_africa/consequences-israeli-blockade-gaza-69870.

Richard Spencer. "Gaza Aid Flotilla: What Is the Blockade and Why Did Israel Impose It? *Telegraph*. https://www.telegraph.co.uk/news/worldnews/middleeast/israel/7790864/Gaza-aid-flotilla-what-is-the-blockade-and-why-did-Israel-impose-it.html.

OPPOSING
VIEWPOINTS®
SERIES

CHAPTER 2

Is the Blockade of the Gaza Strip Legal?

Chapter Preface

The legality of the Israeli blockade of Gaza is important in theory only. The United Nations has proven unable to make a major difference in the region since Israel become a state in 1948. No international court boasts the power to sway either side of this quagmire to change its course of action. And the court of public opinion means little to Hamas or the Israeli government as the blockade extends into a second decade.

But the legal issue does inspire the expression of opinion. And those opinions when heard or read by Palestinians or Israelis and their leaders just might make a difference. The problem is that few minds are being changed. Those that believed ten years ago that the blockade was illegal still feel the same way. Those that felt a decade back that it was legal have also not altered their thinking.

This is likely true for the authors of the viewpoints in this chapter. The issue of the blockade inspires strong views that are not easily swayed. Those that contend that it is illegal cite the humanitarian crisis they perceive that it has caused and that the two sides are not at war. Those that claim the blockade is legal state that Hamas, not Israel, is in control of the Palestinians in Gaza and that the government is simply working to prevent a hostile faction from destroying their very existence. They also assert that Israel is indeed at war with Hamas and that it is nevertheless providing humanitarian aid to the people.

The legality of any government action that affects millions can be based on historical events. Some of the authors in this chapter cite previous blockades to strengthen their points. But each blockade is unique in motivation and execution. The legal ramifications of how Israel is carrying out its blockade of Gaza will continue to be argued until the blockade is over.

> "*The organizers of the Gaza-bound ships have consistently refused to allow their cargo to be inspected, which seems to prove that their humanitarian aid is just a pretext, and their real aim is simply to break the blockade.*"

The Blockade Is Justified from a Legal Standpoint

Alex Safian

In the following viewpoint Alex Safian argues that Israel boasted the legal justification to establish a blockade of Gaza based on international law. He also states that the country has showed a humanitarian side by not fully exercising those rights when they allowed food and medical supplies to reach the Palestinian residents of Gaza. The amount of humanitarian aid that Israel has allowed to reach the area has been a bone of contention among many of the writers contributing to this book. Safian is the associate director of the Committee for Accuracy in Middle East Reporting in America (CAMERA). He has written and lectured extensively about the region.

"Israel's Right to Blockade Gaza and to Interdict Shipping", by Alex Safian, Committee for Accuracy in Middle East Reporting in America, May 31, 2010. Available at: https://www.camera.org/article/israel-146-s-right-to-blockade-gaza-and-to interdict-shipping/. Reprinted by permission.

As you read, consider the following questions:

1. Why does the author believe an organization such as CAMERA became necessary?
2. What kind of opinion does the author express about the humanitarian efforts of the Israeli government?
3. Does the author touch upon the key issue of accepting Israel's right to exist?

Under international law Israel is within its rights to establish a maritime blockade of the Gaza Strip, since Gaza is ruled by Hamas, a hostile terrorist entity that has launched missiles into Israel targeting and killing civilians, and has also infiltrated and attempted to infiltrate into Israel in order to carry out attacks. There is therefore a state of armed conflict between Hamas-ruled Gaza and the State of Israel, and in such a situation Israel is permitted, with certain limitations, to blockade the territory of its adversary.

Israel is actually not fully exercising its blockade rights, since it is allowing inspected food, fuel and other essential materials from Israel into Gaza via trucks. However, Israel has announced that ships attempting to transport supposedly humanitarian supplies into Gaza would have to first dock in Israel for the supplies to be inspected, after which legitimate humanitarian supplies would be trucked into Gaza.

The organizers of the Gaza-bound ships have consistently refused to allow their cargo to be inspected, which seems to prove that their humanitarian aid is just a pretext, and their real aim is simply to break the blockade. Whatever their aim however, Israel has a right under international law to prevent such ships from reaching Gaza.

Even Reuters, not exactly known as a pro-Israel news source, published a brief analysis (Q&A-Is Israel's naval blockade of Gaza legal?) based on interviews with legal experts, and concluded that Israel was well within its rights to declare and enforce a blockade on Gaza. This included, according to the Reuters article, intercepting and boarding ships in international waters: "Under the law of a blockade, intercepting a vessel could apply globally so long as a ship is bound for a "belligerent" territory, legal experts say."

Such blockades have long been part of customary and even conventional international law, and the relevant legal doctrines were reviewed and codified in the San Remo Manual on International Law Applicable to Armed Conflicts at Sea, of 12 June 1994.

The Legal Doctrine of Blockades

Under the San Remo Manual and the laws that it codifies, blockades are a legitimate tool in armed conflicts. Of particular relevance here, paragraph 98 states that merchant vessels that attempt to run a blockade can be not just boarded but actually attacked, ie fired upon:

> 98. Merchant vessels believed on reasonable grounds to be breaching a blockade may be captured. Merchant vessels which, after prior warning, clearly resist capture may be attacked.

Though within its rights to attack the vessels, Israel did not do so. Instead it put its own soldiers at risk in trying to board and take control of the ships.

Here is the relevant portion of the full section on blockades:

SECTION II : METHODS OF WARFARE
    Blockade
    93. A blockade shall be declared and notified to all belligerents and neutral States.
    94. The declaration shall specify the commencement, duration, location, and extent of the blockade and the period within which vessels of neutral States may leave the blockaded coastline.
    95. A blockade must be effective. The question whether a blockade is effective is a question of fact.
    96. The force maintaining the blockade may be stationed at a distance determined by military requirements.
    97. A blockade may be enforced and maintained by a combination of legitimate methods and means of warfare

provided this combination does not result in acts inconsistent with the rules set out in this document.

98. Merchant vessels believed on reasonable grounds to be breaching a blockade may be captured. Merchant vessels which, after prior warning, clearly resist capture may be attacked.

99. A blockade must not bar access to the ports and coasts of neutral States.

100. A blockade must be applied impartially to the vessels of all States.

101. The cessation, temporary lifting, re-establishment, extension or other alteration of a blockade must be declared and notified as in paragraphs 93 and 94.

102. The declaration or establishment of a blockade is prohibited if:

(a) it has the sole purpose of starving the civilian population or denying it other objects essential for its survival; or

(b) the damage to the civilian population is, or may be expected to be, excessive in relation to the concrete and direct military advantage anticipated from the blockade.

103. If the civilian population of the blockaded territory is inadequately provided with food and other objects essential for its survival, the blockading party must provide for free passage of such foodstuffs and other essential supplies, subject to:

(a) the right to prescribe the technical arrangements, including search, under which such passage is permitted; and

(b) the condition that the distribution of such supplies shall be made under the local supervision of a Protecting Power or a humanitarian organization which offers guarantees of impartiality, such as the International Committee of the Red Cross.

104. The blockading belligerent shall allow the passage of medical supplies for the civilian population or for the wounded and sick members of armed forces, subject to the right to prescribe technical arrangements, including search, under which such passage is permitted.

In addition, under Section IV, paragraph 60 (e) enemy merchant vessels become a legitimate military target after refusing an order to stop or actively resisting visit, search or capture;

This is exactly what the Gaza-bound vessels did, thereby rendering themselves military targets.

If one argues that they were not enemy vessels since they were not flying the Hamas flag, they would still be covered under the sections of San Remo regarding neutral vessels:

SECTION V : NEUTRAL MERCHANT VESSELS AND CIVIL AIRCRAFT

Neutral merchant vessels

67. Merchant vessels flying the flag of neutral States may not be attacked unless they:

(a) are believed on reasonable grounds to be carrying contraband or breaching a blockade, and after prior warning they intentionally and clearly refuse to stop, or intentionally and clearly resist visit, search or capture;

(b) engage in belligerent acts on behalf of the enemy;

There is therefore no doubt that Israel was well within its rights to establish and enforce the blockade, including boarding and taking over the Gaza-bound ships in international waters. Israel would even be within its rights to attack such ships if they refused orders to change course away from Gaza.

> *"The Israeli occupation authorities and officials, including Netanyahu, keep describing the siege as legal and claim that it is imposed within international law. Such claims are based on the lie that the Israeli Navy is stopping weapons from getting to the Palestinian resistance groups."*

There Is Nothing Legal About Israeli Aggression

Motasem A. Dalloul

In the following viewpoint Motasem A. Dalloul argues that the Israeli blockade of Gaza represents an illegal occupation. He also cites a number of hostile acts perpetrated by the Israeli government and military against the Palestinian people. He writes about what he describes as seizures of ships by the Israelis intending to dispatch humanitarian aid to the Palestinians and describes Gaza as an open-air prison. Dalloul is a journalist for the Middle East Monitor, *as well as a lecturer about topics relevant to the region.*

"Israel's Siege of Gaza Is Anything but Legal," by Motasem A Dalloul, *Middle East Monitor*, August 07, 2018. Reprinted by permission.

As you read, consider the following questions:

1. Could the author have been more unbiased in this viewpoint?
2. Does he make strong points in expressing his views about a lack of humanitarianism on the part of Israel, or can they be easily disputed?
3. How does the author use events on the high seas to assert that Israeli does not care about the Palestinian people?

O n Sunday 29 July, Israeli commandos boarded a boat taking part in a Freedom Flotilla which was taking humanitarian aid to the besieged Gaza Strip. The boat—Al-Awda (The Return) —was captured by Israel while sailing in international waters. If anyone else had conducted the raid, it would have been condemned as an act of piracy on the high seas. Instead, Israel stopped the much-needed aid going to the 2 million Palestinians in what has been described as an open-air prison.

Twenty humanitarian activists from around the world were on board Al-Awda. They have since reported that they were humiliated and beaten by the Israelis who captured them. Yonatan Shapira, a former Israeli Air Force officer who was on board the boat, said that the commandos beat them up, tasered several people and stole most of the passengers' and crew's property.

Commenting on the attack, the Israeli military tweeted: "The boat was tracked and stopped in accordance with international law." Israeli Prime Minister Benjamin Netanyahu hailed the commandos for "their determined and efficient action in detaining the passengers on the [Al-Awda] ship that tried to reach the Gaza coast in contravention of the law."

Last Saturday, 4 August, at dawn, Israeli commandos raided and seized another boat in the Freedom Flotilla, which was also on its way to deliver medical aid to the coastal enclave, which has been under a tight Israeli-led blockade for 12 years. The siege has resulted in severe shortages of medicines, medical equipment and medical disposals that all hospitals and patients, including those in besieged Gaza, depend on.

Yet again, the Israelis claimed that the ship "was monitored and intercepted in accordance with international law." They added that the ship's passengers were told that they "violated the legal naval blockade" imposed on Gaza.

The Israeli occupation authorities and officials, including Netanyahu, keep describing the siege as legal and claim that it is imposed within international law. Such claims are based on the lie that the Israeli Navy is stopping weapons from getting to the Palestinian resistance groups. Their resistance to Israel's military occupation, by the way, is entirely legitimate according to international laws and conventions.

The reality on the ground is that Israel is blockading 2 million Palestinians in Gaza and tightening restrictions in order that they might take to the streets and overthrow Hamas. This is what the Western-backed Palestinian Authority did in the occupied West Bank, with the help of the Israeli occupation forces, in 2007, shortly after the Islamic Resistance Movement won the "free and fair" democratic elections across the occupied Palestinian territories.

International organisations were prompted to investigate the legality of the Israeli siege by a 2010 attack by commandos on another Freedom Flotilla. Nine Turkish nationals were killed by the Israeli troops as they sailed to Gaza in an attempt to break the siege and deliver vital humanitarian aid; a tenth died later of his injuries. Yet again, the Israeli attack took place in international waters; yet again, it had all the hallmarks of an act of piracy on the high seas.

Throughout the 12 years of the Israeli siege on Gaza, many UN officials and human rights groups have described what the Israeli occupation is doing in and to Gaza as illegal and a flagrant violation of international law. In 2010, the International Committee of the Red Cross (ICRC) said that the blockade of Gaza violates the Geneva Conventions and called for it to be ended.

"The whole of Gaza's civilian population is being punished for acts for which they bear no responsibility," said the ICRC in a five-page statement. "The closure therefore constitutes a collective punishment imposed in clear violation of Israel's obligations under international humanitarian law."

The Head of ICRC Operations for the Middle East, Beatrice Megevand-Roggo, commented, "We are urging Israel to put an end to this closure and call upon all those who have an influence on the situation, including Hamas, to do their utmost to help Gaza's civilian population."

Following the ICRC statement, a panel of five independent UN rights experts reported to the UN Human Rights Council, stressing that the Israeli blockade on the coastal enclave had subjected Gazans to collective punishment in "flagrant contravention of international human rights and humanitarian law." The UN Mission, which investigated the Israeli blockade on Gaza and found it was imposed as a result of the Palestinians participating in free elections, said: "The Mission considers that one of the principal motives behind the imposition of the blockade was a desire to punish the people of the Gaza Strip for having elected Hamas. The combination of this motive and the effect of the restrictions on the Gaza Strip leave no doubt that Israel's actions and policies amount to collective punishment as defined by international law."

The UN Office for the Coordination of Humanitarian Affairs (UNOCHA) and the United Nations Relief and Works Agency (UNRWA) have also said that the siege is illegal. UNOCHA called it "collective punishment, a violation of international humanitarian law," while the former UN High Commissioner for Human Rights, Navi Pillay, stated that it "is illegal and should be lifted."

All of this makes it very clear that Netanyahu and his cronies are lying when they claim that the siege of Gaza is legal. So too are members of the pro-Israel Lobby in world capitals as they seek to influence politicians, aided and abetted by a compliant mainstream media.

Anna Dressler, a Swedish activist who was on board Al-Awda, described Gaza accurately when she said that it is a place where human rights laws seem to have been forgotten. "I believe that every person can change the world, in their own way, wherever they are and in whatever way they can," she added. "Let's start here, with a blockade that should never have existed and yet continues, along with all other man-made catastrophes."

According to Yonatan Shapira, those of his former colleagues in the Israeli armed forces who are blocking the efforts to break the siege should really think about what they will tell their grandchildren in years to come. "Don't think about what your friends will say about you today, think about your grandchildren. Refuse to take part in this ongoing war crime. Refuse to continue murdering people who are locked in the biggest prison in the world. I was once one of you and I know that among you there are some who can still think. Refuse to be the guards of the Gaza ghetto."

"*The relations between Israel and Hamas (which has ruled the Gaza Strip since 2007) are in the nature of armed conflict, meaning that the rules of the laws of armed conflict apply. This means that Israel may control shipping headed for Gaza.*"

The Blockade Would Hold Up in International Court

Ruth Lapidoth

In the following viewpoint Ruth Lapidoth contends that the situation that exists between Israel and Hamas constitutes war, making the blockade of the Gaza strip and interdiction of entering ships quite legal. Lapidoth does not delve into the humanitarian aspect of the blockade, but rather only the legal ramifications, though she does offer her view that Israel is not in control of Gaza and therefore not an occupier. Lapidoth is a professor emeritus of International Law at Hebrew University in Jerusalem and the recipient of the 2006 Israel Prize in Legal Research.

"The Legal Basis of Israel's Naval Blockade of Gaza," by Ruth Lapidoth, Jerusalem Center for Public Affairs, July 18, 2010. Reprinted by permission.

As you read, consider the following questions:

1. How does the author's legal expertise strengthen the claims she makes in this article?
2. Does the author show any bias, or does she offer all her opinions based on proven facts?
3. What are the author's expressed feelings about the motivations of Hamas?

The relations between Israel and Hamas are in the nature of armed conflict. Nowadays no formal declaration of war is needed. Hence the rules of the laws of armed conflict apply. This means that Israel may control shipping headed for Gaza—even when the vessels are still on the high seas.

The rules of naval warfare have not been fully codified in a treaty and are in the nature of binding customary rules. They can be found in the relevant manuals of Western armies (in particular the U.S. and Britain) and in the San Remo Manual prepared by a group of experts.

In order to be legal, a blockade has to be declared and announced, effective, non-discriminatory, and has to permit the passage of humanitarian assistance to the civilian population. In addition, the San Remo Manual of 1994 includes two conditions: first, the state which applies the blockade may decide where and when and through which port the assistance should reach the coast. In addition, the state may require that a neutral organization on the coast should verify who is the recipient of the assistance. In Gaza, for instance, does it reach the civilians or Hamas?

A ship that clearly intends to breach the blockade may be stopped already when it is still on the high seas. Stopping the flotilla heading for Gaza in international waters 100 kilometers from Israel was not illegal; in time of armed conflict, ships intending to breach the blockade may be searched even on the high seas.

Israel is within its rights and is in full compliance with international law because it has fulfilled all of the above-mentioned conditions for a lawful blockade. E.g., in January 2009 Israel notified the relevant authorities of its intention to establish a blockade of the Gaza coast.

What is the legal basis of Israel's naval blockade of Gaza? The relations between Israel and Hamas (which has ruled the Gaza Strip since 2007) are in the nature of armed conflict, meaning that the rules of the laws of armed conflict apply. This means that Israel may control shipping headed for Gaza—even when the vessel is still on the high seas. Israel may not do so in the territorial sea of a third country, such as Cyprus, but in time of armed conflict Israel may check vessels on the high seas that are headed for Gaza.

A naval blockade means preventing the passage (entry or exit) of all vessels to or from the ports and coastal areas of the enemy, irrespective of the kind of cargo carried by these vessels. One has to define clearly the borders of the area to which the blockade applies. The blockade has to be distinguished from other institutions of naval warfare, such as exclusion zones and security zones.

The Sources of International Law on Blockades

What are the sources of international law on blockades? The rules on blockades are based on customary international law, as there is no comprehensive international treaty on this subject. Customary law is binding in international law. According to Article 38 of the Statute of the International Court of Justice, the sources of international law are: a) international treaties, b) international custom, and c) general principles of law recognized by civilized nations. A binding customary rule is created when many states have for a long time behaved in a certain way and have done so because they felt an obligation to behave in that manner.

Blockades have been in existence for hundreds of years. They were mentioned specifically in the 1856 Declaration of Paris (after the Crimean War) Respecting Maritime Law. A more detailed text followed in 1909—the London Declaration on Naval Warfare. This declaration sought to codify the rules of war at sea, but the states that participated in the declaration never ratified it. However, states actually followed the rules laid down in the declaration, and thus its provisions became binding customary rules.

The customary rules on blockade can be found in the manuals of the laws of war issued by certain Western countries such as the United States and Britain. In addition, there is a manual prepared by an international group of experts in 1994 called the San Remo Manual. (While some speak about the San Remo Agreement, there was no agreement, but rather a manual.) In addition, the general principles of the laws of armed conflict apply also to naval warfare.

When Is a Blockade Legal?

In order to be legal, several conditions have to be fulfilled. The first is the requirement to give widespread notice when a blockade is applied and to make sure that any ship that is stopped knows that there is a blockade. Nowadays the problem of notification is much easier than in the past because of the great improvement in communications.

Another condition for the legality of a sea blockade is effectiveness. It is not enough simply to declare a blockade. It has to be enforced, otherwise it is not valid and legal.

According to a further condition, a blockade should not cut off an unrelated foreign state from access to the sea. In the case of Gaza, the blockade does not prevent Egypt from reaching the sea.

Furthermore, a blockade has to be based on equality: It must apply to everybody. Of course there is always the possibility that the blockading party may give special permission to certain neutral ships to go through, but these are exceptions.

A blockade has to permit the passage of humanitarian assistance if needed. However, the San Remo Manual includes two conditions (in Article 103): first, the blockading party may decide where and when and through which port the assistance should reach the coast. In addition, the state may require that a neutral organization on the coast should control the distribution of the items. For instance, in Gaza, does it reach the civilians or Hamas?

Finally, there is the condition that a state may not starve the civilian population (San Remo, Article 102). This conforms also to the general principles of the laws on armed conflict.

What If a Ship Disobeys the Blockade?

What may be done to a ship that disobeys the blockade? Here, there may be a distinction between merchant ships and warships. A merchant ship may be visited, searched, or captured; and if the ship resists, it may be attacked. The situation of neutral warships is not quite clear: Warships may also be searched and captured, but opinions are divided on whether they may be attacked. An attack is certainly permitted in a situation of self-defense.

A ship that clearly intends to breach the blockade can be dealt with while it is still on the high seas. Stopping the flotilla in international waters 100 kilometers from Israel was legal: In time of armed conflict, ships breaching the blockade may be searched even on the high seas.

Precedents of Blockades

There are numerous precedents of blockades. During the Korean War between 1950 and 1953 there was a blockade. In 1971, when Bangladesh tried to secede from Pakistan, India applied a blockade. During the Iran-Iraq war between 1980 and 1988, there was a blockade of the Shatt el-Arab. Lebanon was blockaded for several months in the 2006 war between Israel and Hizbullah, and Israel allowed safe passage from Lebanon to Cyprus for humanitarian purposes.

In the treatment of the flotilla heading for Gaza, Israel has acted in compliance with international law because it has fulfilled all the conditions for a lawful blockade. In January 2009 Israel notified the relevant authorities of its blockade of Gaza—a lawful means of naval war. The existence of an armed conflict between Israel and Hamas in Gaza was well known and did not need a special declaration to that effect.

THE PALMER REPORT

In September 2011, the UN released the so-called Palmer Report on Israel's attack against the Freedom Flotilla in May 2010. The report deemed Israel's blockade legal, however it was widely considered to be a politicized whitewash and contained the crucial caveat that "its conclusions can not be considered definitive in either fact or law."

Also in September 2011, shortly after the Palmer Report was released, an independent UN panel of experts released a report concluding that Israel's blockade of Gaza does indeed violate international law, stating that it amounts to collective punishment in "flagrant contravention of international human rights and humanitarian law." In reference to Palmer, the independent experts wrote:

In pronouncing itself on the legality of the naval blockade, the Palmer Report does not recognize the naval blockade as an integral part of Israel's closure policy towards Gaza which has a disproportionate impact on the human rights of civilians.

Human rights organizations such as Amnesty International and the International Committee of the Red Cross also consider the blockade and siege to be acts of collective punishment that contravene international law.

But Gaza Is Not a State

Can Gaza be considered an enemy although it is not a state? According to international law, this is possible. In any case, according to various judgments of Israel's Supreme Court, the conflict with Gaza is an international conflict and not an internal one because Gaza is not part of Israel. Neither Gaza nor the West Bank have been annexed by Israel, nor has Israel's "law, jurisdiction and administration" been extended thereto (as was done with east Jerusalem in 1967 and the Golan Heights in 1981).

With regard to the status of Gaza: the territory was under Ottoman sovereignty from 1517 until 1917, and then it became part of the British Mandate for Palestine. In 1948 Britain left the

A 2009 Amnesty International report following Operation Cast Lead, Israel's devastating military assault on Gaza in the winter of 2008-9, stated:

The prolonged blockade of Gaza, which had already been in place for some 18 months before the current fighting began, amounts to collective punishment of its entire population. The Fourth Geneva Convention specifically prohibits collective punishment. Its Article 33 provides: "No protected person may be punished for an offence he or she has not personally committed. Collective penalties and likewise all measures of intimidation or of terrorism are prohibited."

A June 2010 statement issued by the International Committee of the Red Cross entitled Gaza closure: not another year! noted:

The whole of Gaza's civilian population is being punished for acts for which they bear no responsibility. The closure therefore constitutes a collective punishment imposed in clear violation of Israel's obligations under international humanitarian law.

"Israel's Blockade of Gaza: Is it Legal?" The Institute for Middle East Understanding, June 14, 2012.

area and Gaza was occupied by Egypt, but Egypt never annexed it. In 1967 Gaza was occupied by Israel, which also did not annex it. In 2005 Israel withdrew from Gaza, and in 2007 it was completely taken over by Hamas. Some say that Gaza is an area sui generis, which means a special situation, while according to others, it is a self-governing territory with certain powers but not with all the powers of a state.

In both the 1993 Israeli-Palestinian Declaration of Principles on Interim Self-Government Arrangements and the 1995 Israeli-Palestinian Interim Agreement on the West Bank and the Gaza Strip, it was agreed that after a certain period of time negotiations would take place on the permanent status of Gaza and the West

Bank, but these negotiations have so far failed. The 2003 Roadmap, to which both parties have agreed, foresees a two-state solution, and that a Palestinian state should be established by agreement with Israel.

Is Israel Still an Occupier?

A recurring question is whether Gaza is still occupied or not. Some say that since Israel is still in control of Gaza's airspace and adjacent sea, Israel is still the occupier. According to another opinion, under the Hague Regulations of 1907 (Respecting the Laws and Customs of War on Land), occupation has to include full control of the area. ("Territory is considered occupied when it is actually placed under the authority of the hostile army. The occupation extends only to the territory where such authority has been established and can be exercised."—Article 42), and of course Israel does not control the whole territory of Gaza. Therefore, it is not responsible for what happens there.

In my opinion, since Israel is not in control of Gaza, it is not the occupier, but in those areas in which Israel still has control —which means sea and airspace—Israel is responsible. Here we have to distinguish between full control of the territory and control only of the sea and airspace.

> *"Although blockades are permitted when carried out in a manner consistent with international law, when they do constitute an international crime, it is critical for the international community to accurately recognize and name it as such."*

The Use of Blockades Can Constitute Crimes Against Humanity

Junteng Zheng

In the following viewpoint Junteng Zheng does not specifically focus on the Israeli blockade of Gaza, but rails against blockades in general as a breach of international law and a crime against humanity. He cites several cases, including that of the Israelis against the Palestinians, in making his point. The author details what he sees as inhumane acts stemming from such blockades and offers his opinion that international courts should deal with the illegality of blockades and be given the power to shut them down. Junteng Zheng is an attorney of international criminal law and human rights in New York City.

"Unlawful Blockades as Crimes Against Humanity", by Junteng Zheng, The American Society of International Law, April 10, 2018. Reprinted by permission.

As you read, consider the following questions:

1. What is the "Rome Statute," and how does the author use it to make his arguments?
2. What other blockades does Junteng Zheng cite here besides the one of Gaza?
3. What arguments does the author use to make his claim that blockades in general are inhumane?

In December 2017, top officials of multiple UN agencies issued a joint statement, warning that the blockade of Yemen could lead to "one of the largest famines in modern times." The International Committee of the Red Cross (ICRC) reported that the blockade was hindering imports food, medicine, and fuel, and the risk of cholera was on the rise.[1] A blockade is a method of warfare that has long been used, but without much international legal scrutiny. To be clear, the use of blockades in armed conflicts is not unlawful per se, but they must be utilized in a manner consistent with international law. This Insight examines under what circumstances the use of blockades can constitute crimes against humanity.

Why "Crimes Against Humanity"?

Modern treaty-based international humanitarian law (IHL) focuses on states' responsibility. It prohibits deliberate starvation as a war tactic in international armed conflicts (IACs)[2] and in some non-international armed conflicts (NIACs).[3] Denying humanitarian access is prohibited under Geneva Convention IV, which only governs IACs.[4] Additional Protocol II leaves it subject to the consent of state(s) concerned and does not mandate such obligation in NIACs[5]—consequently, violating this rule is generally not considered a "grave breach" that entails criminal responsibility.

Customary IHL, governing both state and non-state actors, prohibits deliberate starvation and impediment of humanitarian relief, regardless of conflict classification.[6] Though even when the violations constitute war crimes under customary international law, the key obstacle to accountability is finding a court with proper jurisdiction. The Rome Statute of the International Criminal Court (ICC) explicitly lists starvation and barring humanitarian relief as prosecutable war crimes when committed in IACs but is silent as to NIACs.[7] Due to this jurisdiction limitation, starvation and impediment of humanitarian relief are unlikely to be prosecuted as war crimes before the ICC when committed in NIACs.

This leaves an impunity gap in punishing blockades that cause mass starvation and deprivation of humanitarian relief; however, prosecuting such circumstances as crimes against humanity potentially offers a solution. First, crimes against humanity can be charged regardless of whether there is an armed conflict, or whether it is an IAC or a NIAC. Second, while some relevant actors might not be states parties to the ICC, establishing the commission of crimes against humanity opens the door for a Security Council referral, without having to tackle jurisdictional limit on prosecutable war crimes before the ICC. Third, crimes against humanity can be prosecuted using universal jurisdiction—responsible individuals can be prosecuted before any court (international, regional, or national) with jurisdiction over crimes against humanity.

Undoubtedly, blockades that cause mass starvation and deprivation of humanitarian relief can constitute both war crimes and crimes against humanity. Their prosecution is not mutually exclusive. The conviction of either is also not superior to the other. And blockades do not necessarily entail mass starvation or lack of humanitarian relief. The following sections examine under what circumstances a blockade would constitute crimes against humanity.

Applicable Law and Analysis

Crimes against humanity refer to certain acts "when committed as part of a widespread or systematic attack directed against any civilian population, with knowledge of the attack."[8] The specific punishable "acts" are listed in Article 7(1), among which "extermination" and "other inhumane acts" are relevant to our discussion.

"Extermination"

The Rome Statute defines "attack" as "course of conduct involving the multiple commission of acts referred to in paragraph 1 [of article 7]." Extermination includes "infliction of conditions of life, inter aliathe deprivation of access to food and medicine, calculated to bring about the destruction of part of a population."[9] The key issue is whether imposing blockades can amount to an "attack" for these purposes, and thus constitute "extermination."

An "attack" can be perpetrated as an affirmative violent act or as a result of legislation and government policy.[10] It does not have to be a "military attack"—"any mistreatment of the civilian population" could suffice, including non-violent acts. [11] Particularly, extermination can be committed "either directly, such as by killing the victim with a firearm orless directly, by creating conditions provoking the victim's death."[12] As M. Cherif Bassiouni echoed: extermination could occur with either a kinetic act of "firing a rifle or wielding a knife" or imposing "conditions of life amenable to mass killing."[13]

This interpretation is coherent, read together with the text of the Rome Statute, because other acts of non-violent/non-kinetic nature are also enumerated in Article 7 as punishable acts, like imposing apartheid or pressuring civilians to act in a particular manner.[14] In fact, the "Elements of Crimes" goes even further and includes "omission" as a form of "attack."[15] As such, whether an act constitutes an "attack" under crimes against humanity is determined on the essence of its nature and impact upon civilians, rather than whether it is violent/kinetic at its appearance.

With respect to a blockade, the fact that restrictions of resources themselves were not kinetic acts does not mean they fall outside the meaning of an "attack" for purposes of crimes against humanity. The acts of embargo, when conducted in a manner that cause deprivation of resources indispensable to survival, including food, medicine, sanitation, electricity, and fuel, among others—could constitute an attack. While such deprivation did not instantly translate into deaths, it imposed excessive burdens upon civilians that eventually caused great loss of life. The duration of time between the infliction of conditions and the death is irrelevant for establishing the offense.

The less clear issue is whether the intent—"bring about the destruction of part of a population"—is met. The mental element has two parts: for a crime that requires conduct, the perpetrator must intend to engage in the conduct; for a crime that requires a consequence, the perpetrator must mean to cause the consequence orbe aware that it will occur in the ordinary course of events. [16] "Ordinary course" means that it is assessed with an objective standard—the perpetrator's subjective belief is irrelevant. The ICC has adopted a "virtual certainty" test in assessing the foreseeability—the consequence would normally follow in light of the circumstances where the acts were committed. [17]

Under one view, a blockade is only intended to cut off weapons or resources supplied to adversarial military forces, not to target civilians—any impediment of humanitarian access is only incidental harm. This justification was invoked in the Yemen blockade, as well as the Gaza blockade (2007–2010) and the Ghouta blockade (2013–arguably present). However, relevant actors knew of those situations based on intelligence collected—an ordinary person with similar knowledge to relevant actors, in a similar situation, can and should reasonably foresee such consequences if the blockades continue. The mental element is likely to have been met in this context. But ultimately, the outcome of the mental element assessment depends on how the courts will read the "intent" and "virtual certainty" test vis-à-vis blockades.

"Other inhumane acts"

Article 7(1)(k) of the Rome Statute provides a residual category of "[o]ther inhumane acts of similar character intentionally causing great suffering, or serious injury to body or to mental or physical health." Inhumane acts that fall under crimes against humanity may potentially include deprivation of basic food, medical treatment, and minimum sanitary conditions.[18] Famine and breakouts of disease have indeed long been documented in conflicts. But blockades imposed in situations like Yemen, Gaza, or Ghouta would substantially increase the severity and scale of the already existing crisis.

This Insight will next analyze whether an unlawful blockade can meet the general requirements of crimes against humanity, namely the three "chapeau" elements:

1. committed as part of a widespread or systematic attack;
2. directed against any civilian population pursuant to or in furtherance of a State or organizational policy; and
3. committed with knowledge of the attack.

"Widespread or systematic"

The "widespread or systematic" prong has been interpreted as two disjunctive requirements, meaning that with either satisfied, this element is met. "Widespread" refers to the large-scale nature of the attack. It is not to be evaluated with any specific numerical threshold, but on a contextual basis, including the social context, geographical varieties, and so on.[19] "Systematic" refers to the organized nature of the acts and "the improbability of their random occurrence"—typically reflected in a pattern or methodical plan of acts.[20]

A blockade is usually operated in a manner that is both widespread and systematic. It very often covers a large area of territory, affecting a large civilian population (millions have been severely depleted basic living needs in the case of Yemen). The use of blockade also requires well-organized plans to carry out repetitive and continuing restrictions over resources going into the controlled area. Restrictions imposed through a blockade, in their nature, are unlikely to be random occurrence—it requires a methodical mechanism for enforcement.

"State or organizational policy"

This element requires that a state or organization planned to commit an attack, precluding isolated or random individuals' acts. It is satisfied not only when someone actively promotes the policy, but also when someone commits acts envisaged in the policy. [21] It can be by a government or any type of group that has the capacity to carry out the attack—making it possible to hold non-state actors accountable.[22] This, however, does not require the "policy" to have a specific rationale or be formally adopted. It can be implemented by action or inaction, and can be inferred from the circumstances.[23]

A blockade can only be implemented with actions set out in pre-planned policy/guidelines, through forces of a government or non-state group. For example, in Yemen, blockades have been imposed by both a Saudi-led coalition and some local armed groups, though at different scales. The systematic and consistent restrictions of resources on a large scale cannot be achieved through isolated individual acts. Considering the scale, duration, and intensity of blockades, this "chapeau" element is usually met with either clear evidence of policy or at least inference from circumstantial evidence.

"Knowledge of the attack"

The "knowledge of the attack" element requires that perpetrators have knowledge of an attack on the civilian population and that their act is part of the attack, but it does not require perpetrators to fully understand the exact nature or scale of the attack.[24] With the widespread reporting on the crisis in Yemen, one can hardly deny having knowledge of the "attack" and its consequences. Furthermore, relevant actors knew that the blockade occurred in an overall situation of armed conflict, where other attacks against civilians in violation of international law had already occurred. In this context, actors restricting humanitarian relief not only knew of the overarching policy of the blockade, but also of other attacks against civilians and the overall impact.

Conclusion

Although blockades are permitted when carried out in a manner consistent with international law, when they do constitute an international crime, it is critical for the international community to accurately recognize and name it as such. Doing so defends the integrity of international law by acknowledging and condemning violations, and also galvanizes international attention, which can facilitate appropriate responses. Further, it offers legal basis to hold either states or non-state actors accountable when the prohibited acts occur in NIACs or even non-conflict situations. Overall, considering the complexity of the nature of armed conflicts today, establishing the commission of crimes against humanity provides a greater prospect for accountability.

Notes

[1] *Yemen: As Threat of Famine Looms, UN Urges Saudi-Led Coalition to Fully Lift Blockade of Red Sea Ports*, UN News(Dec. 2, 2017), http://www.un.org/apps/news/story.asp?NewsID=58209#.WnOMp2aZPOT; Y*emen: Border Closure Shuts Down Water, Sewage Systems, Raising Cholera Risk*, ICRC (Nov. 17, 2017), https://www.icrc.org/en/document/yemen-border-closure-shuts-down-water-sewage-systems-raising-cholera-risk.

[2] Protocol Additional to the Geneva Conventions, relating to the Protection of Victims of International Armed Conflicts art. 54(1),June 8, 1977, 1125 U.N.T.S. 3.

[3] Protocol Additional to the Geneva Conventions, relating to the Protection of Victims of Non-International Armed Conflicts, art. 14, June 8, 1977, 1125 U.N.T.S. 609 [Additional Protocol II].

[4] Geneva Convention Relative to the Protection of Civilian Persons in Time of War art. 23, Aug. 12, 1949, 75 U.N.T.S. 287.

[5] Additional Protocol II, *supra* note 3, art. 18(2).

[6] *Customary IHL Database, Rules 53, 55*, ICRC, https://ihl-databases.icrc.org/customary-ihl/eng/docs/v1_rul (last visited Apr. 19. 2018).

[7] Rome Statute of the International Criminal Court, arts. 8(2)(b)(xxv), 8(2)(c), 8(2)(e), July 17, 1998, 2187 U.N.T.S. 90 [hereinafter Rome Statute].

[8] *Id*. art. 7(1).

[9] *Id*. art. 7(2).

[10] *See* William Schabas, The International Criminal Court: A Commentary on the Rome Statute(2010).

[11] Prosecutor v. Katanga,ICC-01/04-01/07, Judgment, 1101 (Mar. 7, 2014).

[12] Prosecutor v. Krstić, IT-98-33-T, Judgment, 499 (Aug. 2, 2001); Prosecutor v. Rutaganda, ICTR-96-3-T, Judgment and Sentence, 83–84 (Dec. 6, 1999).

[13] Arguments can be made that creating "conditions of life amenable to mass killing" is by definition "violent" because deaths are caused. Here, Bassiouni noted the subtle difference between: *1. acts that are violent/kinetic on their face* and *2. acts that are essentially violent.* The initial act or policy of placing a blockade in itself is not kinetic, but it can be essentially violent where it creates conditions amenable to killing.

[14] Rome Statute, *supra* note 7, arts. 7(2)(d), 7(2)(h).

[15] Elements of Crimes, International Criminal Court5 (2011), *available at* https://www.icc-cpi.int/NR/rdonlyres/336923D8-A6AD-40EC-AD7B-45BF9DE73D56/0/ElementsOfCrimesEng.pdf.

[16] Rome Statute, *supra* note 7, art. 30.

[17] Prosecutor v. Bemba, ICC-01/05-01/08, Decision, 362 (June 15, 2009).

[18] David Marcus, *Famine Crimes in International Law*, 97 AJIL 245, 271–79 (2003).

[19] International Law Commission, Report on the Work of Its Sixty-Ninth Session, U.N. Doc. A/72/10, ch. IV, 1–63 (2017).

[20] Prosecutor v. Kunarac, Case No. IT-96-23-T & IT-96-23/1-T, Judgment, 429 (Feb. 22, 2001).

[21] Prosecutor v. Bemba, ICC-01/05-01/08, Judgment, 161 (June 15, 2016).

[22] Katanga, *supra* note 14, 1119.

[23] *Id.* 1108–09, 1113.

[24] Elements of Crimes, *supra* note 15, at 9.

Periodical and Internet Sources Bibliography

The following articles have been selected to supplement the diverse views presented in this chapter.

Al Jazeera. "Gaza Blockade: Does It Break International Law?" Al Jazeera, June 30, 2015. https://www.aljazeera.com/programmes/insidestory/2015/06/gaza-blockade-break-international-law-150629203141416.html.

Amnesty International. "Palmer Report Did Not Find Gaza Blockade Legal, Despite Media Headlines." Amnesty International. https://www.amnestyusa.org/palmer-report-did-not-find-gaza-blockade-legal-despite-media-headlines.

Brian Palmer. "Is the Israeli blockade of Gaza against the law?" Slate, June 1, 2010. http://www.slate.com/articles/news_and_politics/explainer/2010/06/is_the_israeli_blockade_of_gaza_against_the_law.html.

Norman J. Finkelstein. "The Gaza blockade is illegal—and so is the use of force to maintain it." Mondoweiss, July 7, 2018. https://mondoweiss.net/2018/07/blockade-illegal-maintain.

Eugene Kontorovich. "The World Discovers the Legality of the Gaza Blockade." *Washington Post*, March 6, 2014. https://www.washingtonpost.com/news/volokh-conspiracy/wp/2014/03/06/the-world-discovers-the-legality-of-the-gaza-blockade.

Neil MacFarquhar and Ethan Bronner. "Report Finds Naval Blockade by Israel Legal but Faults Raid." *New York Times*, September 1, 2011. https://www.nytimes.com/2011/09/02/world/middleeast/02flotilla.html.

Jonathan Saul. "Q&A: Is Israel's Naval Blockade of Gaza Legal?" Reuters, June 2, 2010. https://www.reuters.com/article/us-israel-flotilla-gaza/qa-is-israels-naval-blockade-of-gaza-legal-idUSTRE65133D20100602.

OPPOSING
VIEWPOINTS®
SERIES

CHAPTER 3

Is the Blockade of the Gaza Strip Inhumane?

Chapter Preface

Whether in wartime or getting caught in political feuds, it is the innocent that suffer the most. Such is certainly the case regarding the Palestinian people in Gaza as they struggle to survive the battle between Israel and Hamas. Those that go hungry or lose loved ones to violence do not care if the battle can be defined as war or not. All they know is personal grief.

The combatants argue that their motivations are to prevent a humanitarian crisis. Israel asserts that lifting the blockade would result in a war for their very existence and the possibility of another in a long line of catastrophes for the Jewish people. Hamas and hardline Palestinians contend that Gaza is rightfully their land and that giving in to Israel is akin to accepting second-class citizenship and hardship.

The result is a stalemate. The viewpoints in the following chapter express heartfelt views of authors on one side of the issue or the other. Those that back the blockade claim that the humanitarian issues have been overstated, or they blame Hamas for the treatment of the Palestinians. They believe that Israel has indeed allowed shipments to feed and clothe those in need and that it is Hamas that promotes suffering for political gain. Those that rail against the blockade state simply that it is preventing humanitarian aid from reaching the people and that Israel simply does not care.

And, again, there is little middle ground. In this age of contentious political wrangling, the centrists have been stifled.

> "*The United States should demand an immediate ceasefire from both Israel and Hamas. The US government should condemn Israel's escalation, bombing and collective punishment of civilians just as forcefully as it has condemned Hamas' firing of rockets.*"

The Palestinian People Are Being Punished Unjustly

Marjorie Cohn

In the following viewpoint Marjorie Cohn argues that what she perceives as the overwhelming use of force by the Israeli military against the Palestinian people constitutes a war crime. She particularly criticizes Israeli leader Benjamin Netanyahu as fighting any opportunity to create a peaceful settlement. Cohn also claims that the United States should condemn Israel as forcefully as it has Hamas. Cohn is a professor emerita at the Thomas Jefferson School of Law and former president of the National Lawyers Guild. She also served as an advisory board member of the Veterans for Peace.

As you read, consider the following questions:

1. Does the viewpoint state any consideration about the right of Israel to exist?
2. How does the author feel that Benjamin Netanyahu is affecting the chances to create peace between the Israelis and Palestinians?
3. Does the viewpoint express any path to a solution?

I srael has commenced full-scale warfare on the people of Gaza. The recent tensions began about six weeks ago when Israeli forces abducted 17 Palestinian teenage boys in the occupied West Bank. Then, on June 12, three Israeli teenagers were abducted in the southern West Bank; Israel blamed Hamas. After the three youths were found dead, a group of Israelis tortured and killed a Palestinian teenager in Jerusalem. Finally, on July 7, Israel launched a large military operation dubbed "Operation Protective Edge" in the Gaza Strip.

During the past week, Israel has killed 162 Palestinian civilians and counting, including 34 children. In addition to more than 1,200 Israeli airstrikes, Israel has threatened to launch a ground invasion of Gaza. Israel attacked a center for the mentally and physically disabled in Beit Zahiya, killing three patients and a nurse. In addition, Israel has stepped up demolitions of Palestinian homes, and administrative detentions of Palestinians without charge or trial.

The UN Office for the Coordination of Humanitarian Affairs(OCHA) reported that 77 percent of the people Israel has killed in Gaza were civilians. Although Hamas has launched about 1,000 rockets into Israel in the past week, no Israelis have been killed.

UN High Commissioner for Human Rights Navi Pillay expressed alarm at the Israeli military operations as well as the indiscriminate firing of rockets from Gaza into Israel. "For its part, the Government of Israel must take all possible measures to ensure full respect for the principles of distinction, proportionality and precautions in attack, during the conduct of hostilities, as required by international humanitarian law. In all circumstances, they must avoid targeting civilians," she said. In light of "deeply disturbing reports that many of the civilian casualties, including of children, occurred as a result of strikes on homes," Pillay continued, "serious doubt [has been raised] about whether the Israeli strikes have been in accordance with international humanitarian law and international human rights law."

The principle of distinction forbids deliberate attacks on civilians or civilian objects. The proportionality principle forbids disproportionate and excessive civilian casualties compared to the claimed military advantage gained in the attack. Precaution requires that measures be taken in advance to ensure compliance with the principles of distinction and proportionality, to minimize incidental loss of civilian life, injury to civilians and damage to civilian objects, and requires taking all feasible precautions in the choice of means and methods of warfare.

Collective Punishment by Israel

Headlines in the mainstream media falsely portray an equivalence of firepower between Israelis and Palestinians in Gaza. But Israel's use of force greatly exceeds that of the Palestinians, and the asymmetric warfare continues to escalate. The Obama administration and Congress have condemned the rocket fire into Israel by Hamas and the "deliberate targeting of civilians." But Washington says Israel has a right to defend itself, justifying Israel's bombing campaign in Gaza and blaming Hamas, while minimizing Israel's role in creating and escalating the violence.

Israel's overwhelming use of military force constitutes collective punishment, which is a war crime. The laws of war, also known as international humanitarian law, are primarily found in the Geneva Conventions. Article 33 of the Fourth Geneva Convention, to which Israel is a party, specifically forbids collective punishment. It says, "No protected person [civilian] may be punished for an offense he or she has not personally committed . . . Reprisals against protected persons and their property are prohibited."

Israel's collective punishment of Palestinians in Operation Protective Edge constitutes a deliberate policy to punish the entire population of Gaza. Since the Palestinians concluded a unity agreement between Fatah in the West Bank and Hamas in Gaza in June, Israel has stepped up the construction of illegal Israeli settlements in the West Bank and Jerusalem. Richard Falk, former UN Special Rapporteur on the situation of human rights in the Palestinian territories occupied by Israel since 1967, noted that Israel broke off the peace talks with the Palestinians before the formation of the Palestinian unity agreement.

Israeli Prime Minister Benjamin Netanyahu has blamed Hamas for the kidnapping and killing of the three Israeli teens in order to discredit the new Palestinian unity agreement. In what amounts to a catch-22, Netanyahu has cynically stymied the peace negotiations because, he said, there was no unified voice to speak for the Palestinians. But now that the Palestinians have a unity agreement, Netanyahu is driving a wedge between Fatah and Hamas in an effort to justify and maintain Israel's occupation of Palestinian territory.

The 140 square-mile Gaza Strip, home to 1.7 million people (half of whom are children), is one of the most densely populated areas in the world. It is often described as the world's largest "open air prison," as Israel maintains a tight blockade, restricting all ingress and egress. Since mid-2013, unemployment has dramatically increased and delivery of basic services has decreased. More than 90 percent of the water in Gaza is unsuitable for drinking. The health system is close to collapse, according to the World Health Organization. Last year, the UN Committee on the Rights of the Child reported, "Palestinian children arrested by [Israeli] military and police are systematically subject to degrading treatment, and often to acts of torture." The committee also concluded that Israel's "illegal long-standing occupation" of Palestinian land, continued expansion of "unlawful" Jewish settlements, construction of the barrier wall into the West Bank [found by the International Court of Justice 10 years ago to violate international law], and the confiscation of land and demolition of homes and livelihoods "constitute severe and continuous violations of the rights of Palestinian children and their families."

After Israel's 2008 to 2009 Operation Cast Lead, in which nearly 1,400 Palestinians (82 percent of whom were civilians) and 13 Israelis were killed, a UN Human Rights Council report by a commission headed by Justice Richard Goldstone concluded, "Disproportionate destruction and violence against civilians were part of a deliberate policy [by Israel]."

In its 2009 report, the Public Committee Against Torture in Israel (PCATI) found, "During Operation Cast Lead no type of property was left untouched: residences, hospitals, schools, mosques, factories and agricultural fields were demolished by the IDF."

Israel, according to PCATI, employed "a coherent strategy that incorporated two major elements into the planning of Operation Cast Lead: 1) The implementation of the 'Dahiye Doctrine,' the principal tenet of which was to cause intentional suffering to civilians so that they would bring pressure to bear on those who were fighting against the IDF [Israel Defense Forces], and 2) The 'No Risk' policy, which placed absolute priority on preventing harm to IDF soldiers, even at the cost of greater danger to Palestinian civilians." Israel is apparently pursuing the same policy in Operation Protective Edge.

In 2013, Falk said, "the people of Gaza have endured the unendurable and suffered what is insufferable for six years. Israel's collective punishment of the civilian population in Gaza must end today." He added, "Israel has the responsibility as the Occupying Power to protect the civilian population."

"In circumstances of prolonged occupation and state terrorism," Falk observed, "Hamas is entitled to claim rights of resistance, although their precise contours are not clearly established by international law. Hamas is certainly entitled to act in self-defense within the constraints of international humanitarian law."

International Reaction

On July 12, 2014, the UN Security Council issued a unanimous statement calling for an immediate ceasefire and "de-escalation of the situation, restoration of calm, and reinstitution of the November 2012 ceasefire." That ceasefire ended eight days of bombings of Gaza by Israel that killed 140 Palestinians, and rocket attacks by Hamas along the border that killed five Israelis. In its July 12 statement, the Council expressed "serious concern regarding the crisis related to Gaza and the protection and welfare of civilians on both sides" and called for respect for international humanitarian law, including the protection of civilians.

Hanna Amira, a member of the executive committee of the Palestine Liberation Organization in the West Bank, said of the Council's statement, "This announcement deals with the oppressor and the victim in the same way; it is a general call to end the fighting, without setting any mechanism to end the fighting. What is needed is an end to the aggression against the Palestinian people in Gaza."

The Palestinian Boycott, Divestment and Sanctions (BDS) National Committee has called on "international governments to impose a two-way arms embargo immediately and to suspend bilateral agreements until Israel fully complies with international law." Indeed, US military aid to Israel also violates US law. The Human Rights and Security Assistance Act requires that the United States halt all military aid to Israel because the latter has engaged in a consistent pattern of gross violation of internationally recognized human rights.

"Because collective punishment is a war crime under the Geneva Conventions, [the Palestinian BDS National Committee] urge[s] the international community to pressure Israel to end its all-out military assault aimed against the total population of Gaza, open the Rafah crossing [between Egypt and Gaza] permanently and heed our call for boycotts, divestment and sanctions." Organizations such as the Bill Gates Foundation, the Presbyterian Church USA and the United Methodist Church are divesting from companies that profit from Israel's occupation, including Hewlett Packard, Motorola Solutions and Caterpillar.

"Israel is able to act with utter impunity because of the military, economic and political support it receives from governments around the world," according to Zaid Shuaibi, a spokesperson for the Palestinian BDS National Committee. Indeed, Israel would be unable to carry out its policies of aggression in Gaza without the support of the United States, which gives Israel more than $3 billion per year.

The United States should demand an immediate ceasefire from both Israel and Hamas. The US government should condemn Israel's escalation, bombing and collective punishment of civilians just as forcefully as it has condemned Hamas' firing of rockets. The Gaza blockade and limitations on freedom of travel of Gazans should be lifted and Israel's occupation of the Palestinian territories should be ended.

> *"Israel's illegal air, land and sea blockade of the Gaza Strip entered its 11th year, continuing the long-standing restrictions on the movement of people and goods into and from the area, collectively punishing Gaza's entire population."*

More Than a Decade of Occupation

Amnesty International

In the following viewpoint Amnesty International provides a rundown and analysis of what the organization cites as humanitarian illegalities perpetrated by the Israelis against the Palestinian people. The organization considers the blockade as further evidence that Israel is a military occupier. Amnesty International does cite violence against Israelis by the Palestinians, but its overall slant in this piece is against the actions of the Israeli government. Amnesty International is a human rights organization that focuses its attention and efforts on humanitarian crises throughout the world.

"Israel and Occupied Palestinian Territories," Amnesty International, 2018. Reprinted by permission.

As you read, consider the following questions:

1. How do the goals of Amnesty International as an organization affect the fairness of this viewpoint?
2. What does this viewpoint suggest that Israel do to end what it sees as a humanitarian crisis?
3. What specific incidents are cited aside from the blockade itself to prove that Israel is treating the Palestinian people inhumanely?

June marked 50 years since Israel's occupation of the Palestinian Territories and the start of the 11th year of its illegal blockade of the Gaza Strip, subjecting approximately 2 million inhabitants to collective punishment and a growing humanitarian crisis. The Israeli authorities intensified expansion of settlements and related infrastructure across the West Bank, including East Jerusalem, and severely restricted the freedom of movement of Palestinians. Israeli forces unlawfully killed Palestinian civilians, including children, and unlawfully detained within Israel thousands of Palestinians from the Occupied Palestinian Territories (OPT), holding hundreds in administrative detention without charge or trial. Torture and other ill-treatment of detainees, including children, remained pervasive and was committed with impunity. Israel continued to demolish Palestinian homes in the West Bank and in Palestinian villages inside Israel, forcibly evicting residents. Conscientious objectors to military service were imprisoned. Thousands of African asylum-seekers were threatened with deportation.

Background

Israeli authorities intensified settlement expansion and land appropriation in the OPT. US and international efforts to revive negotiations failed, and Israeli-Palestinian relations remained tense. In January, Israeli authorities passed the so-called "regularization law" that retroactively legalized the settler takeover of thousands of hectares of privately owned Palestinian land and an estimated 4,500 settler homes. In addition, Israeli authorities announced and issued tenders for tens of thousands of new settlement units in East Jerusalem and across the rest of the West Bank.

Palestinians carried out stabbings, car-rammings, shootings and other attacks against Israelis in the West Bank and in Israel. The attacks, mostly carried out by individuals unaffiliated to armed groups, killed 14 Israelis and one foreign national. Israeli forces killed 76 Palestinians and one foreign national. Some were unlawfully killed while posing no threat to life.

In March, the UN Economic and Social Commission for Western Asia issued, then withdrew, a report determining Israel to be "guilty of the crime of apartheid" against Palestinians. In May, a UNESCO resolution reaffirmed the occupied status of East Jerusalem and criticized Israel's conduct in the city. Following the killing of two Israeli policemen by Palestinians, in July Israel installed metal detectors to screen Muslim worshippers entering the Temple Mount/Haram al-Sharif. The new security measures led to heightened tensions and mass protests by Palestinians, including collective prayers, across the West Bank. The prayer protests, often met with excessive force, ended once the metal detectors were removed.

In September, the Hamas de facto administration in Gaza and the "national consensus" government in the West Bank embarked on a reconciliation process, which was rejected by Israel.

In December, US President Donald Trump recognized Jerusalem as Israel's capital in violation of international law, sparking widespread protests across the OPT and globally.

Freedom of Movement—Gaza Blockade and West Bank Restrictions

Israel's illegal air, land and sea blockade of the Gaza Strip entered its 11th year, continuing the long-standing restrictions on the movement of people and goods into and from the area, collectively punishing Gaza's entire population. Combined with

Egypt's almost total closure of the Rafah border crossing, and the West Bank authorities' punitive measures, Israel's blockade triggered a humanitarian crisis with electricity cuts reducing access to electricity from an average of eight hours per day down to as little as two to four hours, affecting clean water and sanitation and diminishing health service access, and rendering Gaza increasingly "unlivable" according to the UN. Gaza's economy deteriorated further and post-conflict reconstruction of civilian infrastructure remained severely hindered; some 23,500 Palestinians remained displaced since the 2014 conflict. Many patients with life-threatening illnesses were unable to access treatment outside Gaza due to Israeli restrictions and delays by West Bank authorities in processing referrals. Israeli forces maintained a "buffer zone" inside Gaza's border with Israel and used live ammunition against Palestinians who entered or approached it, wounding farmers working in the area. Israeli forces also fired at Palestinian fishermen in or near the "exclusion zone" along Gaza's coastline, killing at least one and injuring others.

In the West Bank, Israel maintained an array of military checkpoints, bypass roads and military and firing zones, restricting Palestinian access and travel. Israel established new checkpoints and barriers, especially in East Jerusalem. In response to Palestinian attacks on Israelis, the military authorities imposed collective punishment; they revoked the work permits of attackers' family members and closed off villages and entire areas including Silwad, Deir Abu Mishal and Beit Surik.

In Hebron, long-standing prohibitions limiting Palestinian presence, tightened in October 2015, remained in force. In Hebron's Tel Rumeida neighbourhood, a "closed military zone", Israeli forces subjected Palestinian residents to oppressive searches and prevented the entry of other Palestinians while allowing free movement for Israeli settlers. In May, Israel erected a new checkpoint and a new fence barrier within Hebron's H2 area, arbitrarily confining the Palestinian Gheith neighbourhood and segregating a street alongside the area.

Arbitrary Arrests and Detentions

Israel detained or continued to imprison thousands of Palestinians from the OPT, mostly in prisons in Israel, in violation of international law. Many detainees' families, particularly those in Gaza, were not permitted entry to Israel to visit their relatives.

The authorities continued to substitute administrative detention for criminal prosecution, holding hundreds of Palestinians, including children, civil society leaders and NGO workers, without charge or trial under renewable orders, based on information withheld from detainees and their lawyers. More than 6,100 Palestinians, including 441 administrative detainees, were held in Israeli prisons at the end of the year. Israeli authorities also placed six Palestinian citizens of Israel under administrative detention.

In April around 1,500 Palestinian prisoners and detainees launched a 41-day hunger-strike to demand better conditions, family visits, an end to solitary confinement and administrative detention, and access to education. The Israeli Prison Service punished hunger-striking detainees, using solitary confinement, fines, and denial of family visits.

Palestinians from the West Bank charged with protest-related and other offences faced unfair military trials, while Israeli civilian courts trying Palestinians from East Jerusalem or the Gaza Strip issued harsh sentences even for minor offences.

In April the Israeli High Court of Justice issued a decision to reduce excessive sentencing of Palestinians under the military judicial system and ordered that legislation be amended to apply shorter sentences as of May 2018. Despite the ruling, the sentences would remain harsher than those in the Israeli civilian judicial system.

Khalida Jarrar, a member of the Palestinian Legislative Council and board member of the NGO Addameer, and Addameer staff member Salah Hammouri, remained in administrative detention at the end of the year.

The trial of Mohammed al-Halabi, a Gaza-based humanitarian worker, began at Beer Sheva District Court on charges of embezzlement from the NGO World Vision to fund Hamas. Neither an Australian government review of World Vision Gaza nor an internal World Vision audit found any evidence to support the charges. Mohammed al-Halabi stated in court that he was tortured during interrogation and detention.

Torture and Other Ill-treatment

Israeli soldiers and police and Israel Security Agency officers subjected Palestinian detainees, including children, to torture and other ill-treatment with impunity, particularly during arrest and interrogation. Reported methods included beatings, slapping, painful shackling, sleep deprivation, use of stress positions and threats. No criminal investigations were opened into more than 1,000 complaints filed since 2001. Complaints of torture and other ill-treatment by the Israeli police against asylum-seekers and members of the Ethiopian community remained common.

In December the Israeli High Court of Justice accepted the Attorney General's decision not to open a criminal investigation into Asad Abu Ghosh's torture claims despite credible evidence, thus condoning the continued use of stress positions and sleep deprivation against Palestinian detainees by Israeli interrogators.

Unlawful Killings

Israeli soldiers, police and security guards killed at least 75 Palestinians from the OPT, including East Jerusalem, and five Palestinians with Israeli citizenship. Some of those killed were shot while attacking Israelis or suspected of intending an attack. Many, including children, were shot and unlawfully killed while posing no immediate threat to life. Some killings, such as that of Yacoub Abu al-Qi'an, shot in his car by police in Umm al-Hiran in January, appeared to have been extrajudicial executions.

Excessive Use of Force

Israeli forces, including undercover units, used excessive and sometimes lethal force when they used rubber-coated metal bullets and live ammunition against Palestinian protesters in the OPT, killing at least 20, and injuring thousands. Many protesters threw rocks or other projectiles but were posing no threat to the lives of well-protected Israeli soldiers when they were shot. In July, in response to the tensions over Temple Mount/Haram al-Sharif, the authorities killed 10 Palestinians and injured more than 1,000 during the dispersal of demonstrations, and conducted at least two violent raids on al-Makassed hospital in East Jerusalem. In December, wheelchair user Ibrahim Abu Thuraya was shot in the head by an Israeli soldier as he was sitting with a group of protesters near the fence separating Gaza from Israel.

Freedoms of Expression, Association and Assembly

The authorities used a range of measures, both in Israel and the OPT, to target human rights defenders who criticized Israel's continuing occupation.

In March the Knesset (parliament) passed an amendment to the Entry into Israel Law banning entry into Israel or the OPT to anyone supporting or working for an organization that has issued or promoted a call to boycott Israel or Israeli entities, including settlements. The authorities continued to obstruct human rights workers' attempts to document the situation by denying them entry into the OPT, including the UN Special Rapporteur on the human rights situation in the OPT. An Amnesty International staff member was denied entry after he was questioned about the organization's work on settlements.

Using public order laws in East Jerusalem, and military orders in the rest of the West Bank, Israeli authorities prohibited and suppressed protests by Palestinians, and arrested and prosecuted protesters and human rights defenders. In July, the military trials of Palestinian human rights defenders Issa Amro and Farid al-Atrash began on charges related to their role in organizing peaceful protests against Israel's settlement policies. Israeli authorities continued to harass other Hebron-based human rights activists, including Badi Dweik and Imad Abu Shamsiya, and failed to protect them from settler attacks.

From May to August, the Israeli authorities detained prisoner of conscience and writer Ahmad Qatamesh under a three-month administrative detention order solely on account of his non-violent political activities and writing.

Palestinian human rights NGOs, including Al-Haq, Al Mezan and Addameer, encountered increased levels of harassment by Israeli authorities. Israeli authorities initiated tax investigations against Omar Barghouti, a prominent advocate of the boycott, divestment and sanctions campaign, in what appeared to be an effort to silence his work.

Several Israeli human rights organizations, including Breaking the Silence, Gisha, B'tselem and Amnesty International Israel were also targeted by government campaigns to undermine their work, and faced smears, stigmatization and threats.

Right to Housing—Forced Evictions and Demolitions

In the West Bank, including East Jerusalem, the Israeli authorities carried out a large number of demolitions of Palestinian property, including 423 homes and structures built without Israeli permits that remained virtually impossible for Palestinians to obtain, forcibly evicting more than 660 people. Many of these demolitions were in Bedouin and herding communities that the Israeli authorities planned to forcibly transfer. The authorities also collectively punished the families of Palestinians who had carried out attacks on Israelis, by demolishing or making uninhabitable their family homes, forcibly evicting approximately 50 people.

Israeli authorities forcibly evicted eight members of the Shamasneh family from their home in Sheikh Jarrah, East Jerusalem, allowing Jewish settlers to move in. The authorities also demolished dozens of Palestinian homes inside Israel that they

THE CRUELTY OF THE BLOCKADE

Gaza's 1.5 million people are still suffering from a shortage of construction materials, a ban on exports and severe restrictions on movement six months after Israel agreed to ease its blockade on the territory, according to a report from 21 international organisations.

The loosening of the embargo has done little to improve the plight of Gaza's civilians, according to the coalition, which includes Amnesty, Oxfam, Save the Children, Christian Aid and Medical Aid for Palestinians. It calls for fresh international action to persuade Israel to unconditionally lift the blockade.

Israel agreed to ease its restrictions on goods and materials allowed into Gaza following its attack on a flotilla of aid boats in May, in which nine Turkish activists were killed. Since then the import of food and many other consumer items has resumed, although there is still a ban on exports and severe restrictions on construction materials. Israel argues that the latter could be used by militants for military purposes.

Tony Blair, the representative of the Middle East Quartet of the US, the UN, the EU and Russia, echoed the call for Israel to accelerate its easing of its blockade in an interview at the weekend. "There has been significant change in Gaza, but not nearly as much as we need," he told the Associated Press.

said were built without permits, including in Palestinian towns and villages in the Triangle, the Galilee, and in "unrecognized" Bedouin villages in the Negev/Naqab region. In January the Israeli police forcibly demolished the Bedouin village of Umm al-Hiran, to begin building a Jewish town in its place. The Knesset passed a law in April that raised the fines for building without permits, charging punitive costs for the demolition to those whose homes have been demolished, and limited recourse to the courts for those challenging demolition or eviction orders. In August, the authorities demolished al-Araqib village in the Negev/Naqab for the 116th time. Residents were ordered to compensate the state

According to today's report, Dashed Hopes: Continuation of the Gaza Blockade, imports of construction materials are 11% of the 2007 pre-blockade levels. Despite having agreed to allow in materials for the United Nations Relief and Works Agency to rebuild its schools and clinics damaged or destroyed in the three-week war in 2008-09, Israel has permitted only 7% of the necessary amount.

Many of the thousands of homes and businesses hit during the war are still unrepaired almost two years later because of the shortage of building materials.

Exports remain banned with the exception of strawberries and carnations for European markets. Israel now allows clothing factories to import fabric, but blocks the export of finished items.

But some businesses are still unable to import raw materials they need. According to the report, two-thirds of Gaza's businesses have closed since the blockade was tightened in June 2007, and the rest are operating at restricted capacity.

Israel is maintaining an overall ban on the movement of people, with the number of permits granted to people to leave Gaza less than 1% of the number 10 years ago.

"Israel Accused over 'Cruel' Gaza Blockade," by Harriet Sherwood, *Guardian* News and Media Limited, November 30, 2010.

362,000 new shekels (approximately USD100,000) for the cost of demolition and lawyers' fees.

Impunity

More than three years after the end of the 2014 Gaza-Israel conflict, in which some 1,460 Palestinian civilians were killed, many in evidently unlawful attacks including war crimes, the authorities had previously indicted only three soldiers for looting and obstructing an investigation.

In a rare move, in January an Israeli military court convicted Elor Azaria, a soldier whose apparent extrajudicial execution of a wounded Palestinian in Hebron was filmed, of manslaughter. His conviction and 18-month prison sentence, which was confirmed on appeal but reduced by four months by Israel's military Chief of Staff in September, failed to reflect the gravity of the crime. Israeli authorities failed to investigate, or closed investigations into, cases of alleged unlawful killings of Palestinians by Israeli forces in both Israel and the OPT.

The Prosecutor of the ICC continued her preliminary examination of alleged crimes under international law committed in the OPT since 13 June 2014.

Violence Against Women and Girls

There were new reports of violence against women; Palestinian communities in Israel were particularly affected. In June, the Special Rapporteur on violence against women issued recommendations urging Israeli authorities to carry out law and policy reforms by integrating CEDAW standards; to combat and prevent violence against women in Israel and the OPT; and to investigate reported abuses.

Deprivation of Nationality

On 6 August the Haifa District Court confirmed the citizenship revocation of Alaa Zayoud, who was stripped of his citizenship and rendered stateless by the Minister of the Interior following a conviction for attempted murder. An appeal against the decision was pending before the Supreme Court at the end of the year. The authorities also revoked the citizenship of dozens of Palestinian Bedouin residents of the Negev/Naqab region without process or appeal, leaving them as stateless residents.

Refugees and Asylum-seekers

The authorities continued to deny asylum-seekers, more than 90% of whom were from Eritrea or Sudan, access to a fair or prompt refugee status determination process. More than 1,200 asylum-seekers were held at the Holot detention facility and at Saharonim

Prison in the Negev/Naqab desert at the end of the year. According to activists, there were more than 35,000 asylum-seekers in Israel; 8,588 asylum claims remained pending. In December, the Knesset passed an amendment to the anti-infiltration law that would force asylum-seekers and refugees to accept relocation to countries in Africa or face imprisonment. Tens of thousands were at risk of deportation.

Conscientious Objectors

At least six Israeli conscientious objectors to military service were imprisoned, including Tamar Zeevi, Atalia Ben-Abba, Noa Gur Golan, Hadas Tal, Mattan Helman and Ofir Averbukh. Israeli authorities recognized Tamar Zeevi as a conscientious objector and released her from conscription after she served a total of 100 days in prison.

> "*Any framework for negotiations must
> be multilateral and must involve
> all players.*"

Hamas—not Israel—Is to Blame for the Suffering in Gaza

Noa Landau

In the following viewpoint Noa Landau argues that it is Hamas, not Israel, that controls civilian life in Gaza and has taken on the responsibility of overseeing the well-being or lack thereof of the Palestinian people. Landau writes about efforts made during a meeting of representatives from Israel, the United States, and the Palestinian Authority to ensure that those citizens of Gaza were provided the support they required. Landau is a diplomatic correspondent and head of the news department of Hareetz, *a publication that focuses on issues in the Middle East.*

As you read, consider the following questions:

1. How did the author present the meeting in Brussels?
2. What difference does Israel believe there would be between a Hamas-led government and that of the Palestinian Authority in creating a stable environment?
3. Does the author interject any personal opinion?

"Israel Presents $1 Billion Rehabilitation Plan for Gaza, but Demands Palestinian Authority Take Over," by Noa Landau, *Haaretz* Daily Newspaper Ltd, February 1, 2018. Reprinted by permission.

Representatives of Israel, the Palestinian Authority and the United States participated in an emergency conference in Brussels on Wednesday of countries and organizations that provide financial support for Palestinians.

Israel presented humanitarian assistance plans at the gathering for the rehabilitation of the Gaza Strip with a focus on desalination, electricity and natural gas infrastructure projects in addition to upgrading of the industrial zone at the Erez border crossing with Israel. The total cost of the projects is estimated at a billion dollars, which Israel asked the international community to fund. The plan was first reported by Haaretz.

Regional Cooperation Minister Tzachi Hanegbi, who represented Israel at the conference, presented the plans but noted that carrying them out would require that the PA take responsibility for civilian life in Gaza, which has been under the control of Hamas since the Islamist movement forcefully ousted the PA there in 2007.

The American representative at the gathering, U.S. President Donald Trump's special Middle East envoy, Jason Greenblatt, directed remarks at Palestinian Prime Minister Rami Hamdallah which made reference to Trump's recognition in December of Jerusalem as Israel's capital. Greenblatt said the historical link between the Jewish people and its capital was not disputable and that Trump was simply recognizing a historical reality. Trump had not expressed a position on Jerusalem's borders, its final status or the status quo in the city's holy places, Greenblatt added, and the U.S. president remains committed to advance the peace process. Abandoning peace negotiations will not benefit the parties to the conflict, but the step will mainly harm the Palestinians, Greenblatt added.

The Brussels meeting was also attended by the foreign ministers of Jordan, Egypt and Morocco as well as senior representatives from Tunisia, Saudi Arabia, the United Arab Emirates and Kuwait. The meeting of the group, formally known as the ad hoc liaison committee of the International Donor Group for Palestine, was convened by its current chairwoman, Norwegian Foreign Minister Ine Eriksen Søreide, and the European Union's foreign policy chief, Federica Mogherini.

The meeting was convened against the backdrop of a threat by the U.S. to cut financial assistance to the Palestinians, the deteriorating humanitarian situation in Gaza and the stalled process of reconciliation between Hamas and Fatah, the dominant party in the PA.

The EU's Mogherini called the conference an opportunity for all of the parties involved to sit down together for the first time since the American recognition of Jerusalem as Israel's capital. "The basis and objective of our engagement is and remains the two-state solution, with Jerusalem as future capital of both states, the State of Israel and the State of Palestine. This is a position based on the Oslo Accords and on international law, in particular the relevant UN Security Council resolutions," Mogherini said. "The raison d'etre of the ad hoc liaison committee is and remains the shared objective of a two-state solution."

"Any framework for negotiations must be multilateral and must involve all players, all partners that are essential to this process. A process without one or the other would simply not work, would simply not be realistic," she said, before going on to add: "We need to maintain the political horizon for the two-state solution, as we believe that there is no alternative."

"In the meantime, there are many practical steps that can advance on the ground and we will look at these steps also today: Continue our support for the Palestinian Authority; continue our support for UNRWA [the United Nations Relief and Works Agency for Palestine Refugees]; work for the security of all, because we know that the more progress we can achieve on the ground, the more this can help prevent violence and the more this can also help resume a political process," Mogherini added.

"We believe it is important that the Palestinian Authority is committed to unite the West Bank and Gaza under one single and legitimate authority. And in this regard we strongly support the indispensable Egyptian role and engagement that we value as extremely positive. The political situation in Gaza is directly linked to the security situation in the entire region and to our common fight against terrorism. And we believe Israel's legitimate security concerns must be met, also in that context," the EU's foreign policy chief continued.

"We are thinking first and foremost, obviously, of the population in Gaza. The daily life of citizens has been very difficult for a too long time and this despite large international humanitarian help. We are ready to increase our support if the political conditions are met," she noted.

Mogherini announced a 42.5 million euro ($52.7 million) assistance package for the Palestinians which includes 14.9 million euros for activities in East Jerusalem that an EU statement said would be used "to preserve the Palestinian character of the city." The balance is earmarked for "a democratic and accountable Palestinian State through targeted policy reform." This is in addition to the EU's current 107 million euros in support for UNRWA.

With regard to an American peace plan, Mogherini said: "We will wait and see. For the moment, we do not have details or even a time framework." However, she stated that "For us what counts is that everybody recognizes that the United States [is] essential for any process to realistically have a chance to succeed, but also for our friends in the United States to understand that alone it would be more difficult to achieve anything."

Mogherini said she would shortly invite representatives of the Arab League to meet with her on the Israeli-Palestinian issue under the leadership of Jordan and Egypt.

> "The Israeli occupation of the West
> Bank and Gaza could end in peace,
> with Israel abandoning paranoia and
> racial violence."

Nonviolent Protest Can Bring an End to the Inhumanity

Kathy Kelly

In the following viewpoint Kathy Kelly argues that nonviolent protest and international pressure can end the Gaza blockade. Kelly announces her plan to participate in the 2011 Freedom Flotilla II, a planned event to break the maritime blockade, that ultimately did not happen. The previous year, another Freedom Flotilla had been raided by Israeli forces. This raid attracted international attention, forcing Israel to let up somewhat. The author describes the conditions that have led her to risk her own life and why, ultimately, she insists on optimism. Kelly is co-coordinator of Voices for Creative Nonviolence.

As you read, consider the following questions:

1. What is the significance of the name of the boat the author planned on sailing on?
2. What does "the world watched but did nothing" mean?
3. Why does the author compare Gaza with South Africa?

In late June 2011, I'm going to be a passenger on "The Audacity of Hope," the US boat in this summer's international flotilla to break the illegal and deadly Israeli siege of Gaza. Organizers, supporters and passengers aim to nonviolently end the brutal collective punishment imposed on Gazan residents since 2006 when the Israeli government began a stringent air, naval and land blockade of the Gaza Strip explicitly to punish Gaza's residents for choosing the Hamas government in a democratic election. Both the Hamas and the Israeli governments have indiscriminately killed civilians in repeated attacks, but the vast preponderance of these outrages over the length of the conflict have been inflicted by Israeli soldiers and settlers on unarmed Palestinians. I was witness to one such attack when I was last in Gaza two years ago, under heavy Israeli bombardment in a civilian neighborhood in Rafah.

In January 2009, I lived with a family in Rafah during the final days of the "Operation Cast Lead" bombing. We were a few streets down from an area where there was heavy bombing. Employing its ever-replenished stockpile of U.S. weapons, the Israeli government sought to destroy tunnels beneath the Egyptian border through which food, medicine, badly-needed building supplies, and possibly a few weapons as well were evading the internationally condemned blockade and entering Gaza.

Throughout that terrible assault, Israel pounded civilians in Gaza, turning villages, homes, refugee camps, schools, mosques and infrastructure into rubble. According to a report by the Israeli human rights organization B'Tselem, the attack killed 1,385 Palestinians, nearly a quarter of them minors, with an uncountable number more to succumb, in the months and years following, to malnutrition, disease, and suicidal despair, the consequences of forced impoverishment under a still continuing siege that salts Gaza's dreadful wounds by preventing it from even starting to rebuild.

All I could feel at the time was that the people in the Gaza Strip were horribly trapped, almost paralyzed.

The day of the cease-fire, when the sounds of bombing stopped, my young friends insisted that we must move quickly to visit the Al Shifaa hospital in Gaza City. Doctors there were shaken and stunned, after days of trying to save lives in a hopelessly overcrowded emergency room, with blood pooling at their feet. Dr. Nafez Abu Shabham, head of Al Shifaa's burn unit, put his head in his hands and spoke incredulously to us. "For 22 days, the world watched," he lamented, "and no country tried to stop the killing."

He may well be putting his head in his hands again, today as too many of us have stopped even watching. "Human rights groups in Gaza are urgently requesting international aid groups and donor groups to intervene and deliver urgent medical aid to Palestinian hospitals in Gaza," according to a June 12 Al Jazeera report. "Palestinian officials say that Gaza's medicinal stock is nearly empty and is in crisis. This affects first aid care, in addition to all other levels of medical procedures."

After the attack, I visited the Gaza City dormitory of a young university student with two of his friends. It was a shambles. We sifted through broken glass and debris, trying to salvage some notebooks and texts. Their lives have been like that. They've since graduated but there is no work. "The Gaza Strip enters its fifth year of a full Israeli blockade by land, air and sea with unemployment at 45.2%, one of the highest rates in the world," according to a UN aid agency report. (June 14, 2011). Harvard scholar Sara Roy, in a June 2, 2009 report for Harvard's Crimson Review, noted that:

> Gaza is an example of a society that has been deliberately reduced to a state of abject destitution, its once productive population transformed into one of aid-dependent paupers…After Israel's December [2008] assault, Gaza's already-compromised conditions have become virtually unlivable. Livelihoods, homes, and public infrastructure have been damaged or destroyed on a scale that even the Israel Defense Forces admitted was indefensible. In Gaza today there is no private sector to speak of and no industry.

When the bombing had stopped, we visited homes and villages where the unarmed had been killed. Sabrina Tavernise of the *New York Times* would later verify that, in the village of Al Atatra, IDF soldiers had fired white phosphorous missiles into the home of a woman named Sabah Abu Halemi, leaving her badly burned and burning to death her husband and three of her children. I visited her in the hospital, watching a kindly Palestinian doctor spend his greatly needed time off sitting at her bedside, offering only wordless comfort as she gripped his hand.

We must not turn away from suffering in Gaza.

We must continue trying to connect with Gazans living under siege.

There is some risk involved in this flotilla. The Israeli government threatens to board each ship in the flotilla with snipers and attack dogs. A year ago the Israeli Navy fired on the Turkish ship, the Mavi Marmara, from the air, then documented its passengers' panicked response as their justification for executing nine activists, including one young U.S. citizen, Furkhan Dogan, shot several times in the back and head at close range. It then refused to cooperate with an international investigation.

The Israeli occupation of the West Bank and Gaza, amounting to what is internationally recognized as an apartheid system, could end in peace, with Israel abandoning paranoia and racial violence to allow peace. Apartheid ended in South Africa without the wave of bloodshed and reprisals that its supporters claimed to fear as their excuse for holding on to the wealth and power which their system afforded them. They achieved greater peace and safety for themselves and their children by finding the courage to finally allow peace, safety, and freedom to their neighbors. It's a lesson the U.S. government has all too often missed. This June, the governments of Israel and above all the United States must finally embrace the audacity of hope.

Periodical and Internet Sources Bibliography

The following articles have been selected to supplement the diverse views presented in this chapter.

Moshe Arens. "Opinion: How to Solve the Humanitarian Crisis in Gaza." *Hareetz,* July 18, 2018. https://www.haaretz.com/opinion/.premium-how-to-solve-the-humanitarian-crisis-in-gaza-1.6162864.

Beverly Milton-Edwards. "Gaza Protests Highlight Humanitarian Crisis and Lack of Political Progress to Peace." Brookings, April 5, 2018. https://www.brookings.edu/opinions/gaza-protests-highlight-humanitarian-crisis-and-lack-of-political-progress-to-peace.

Saeb Erekat. "Gaza Is not a Humanitarian Disaster, It Is a Crisis of Human Consciousness That Demands Your Attention." *Newsweek*, March 15, 2018. https://www.newsweek.com/gaza-not-humanitarian-disaster-it-crisis-human-consciousness-demands-your-846528.

Gregory Shupak. "Gaza Does not Have a Humanitarian Crisis. It Has a Colonial Problem." Middle East Eye, February 19, 2018. https://www.middleeasteye.net/columns/gaza-does-not-have-humanitarian-crisis-1481200950.

Ann M. Simmons. "Life in the Gaza Strip—a Cauldron of Deficit, Despair and Desperation." *Los Angeles Times*, February 8, 2018. https://www.latimes.com/world/middleeast/la-fg-global-gaza-humanitarian-situation-20180206-story.html.

Sandy Tolan. "Israel's About-Face on Gaza." *Foreign Policy*, November 21, 2018. https://foreignpolicy.com/2018/11/21/israels-about-face-on-gaza.

United Nations. "Humanitarian Coordinator Warns of Worsening Crisis in Gaza." United Nations, July 17, 2018. https://www.un.org/unispal/document/humanitarian-coordinator-warns-of-worsened-crisis-in-gaza-ocha-press-release.

CHAPTER 4

Can the Problem Be Solved?

Chapter Preface

It falls under the category of the Immovable Force vs. the Unstoppable Object. Hamas vs. Netanyahu. An issue pitting two opposite sides politically that have dug in and shown no desire to compromise cannot be easily solved. Neither Hamas nor the hardline Israeli government has expressed a desire to negotiate without their basic demands being met. It seems Hamas will never give in to the mandate that it ensures Israeli sovereignty, and Israel will continue to refuse to end the blockade without such assurances. One wonders even with that guarantee if Israel will ever allow for a two-state solution and Palestinian freedom.

So there they stand, like the North-Going Zax and South-Going Zax in the Dr. Seuss book, refusing to budge for years and years. Perhaps it will take outside forces such as the United States and Russia, or a joint effort by the usually ineffective United Nations, to broker a peace. But it seems only by force will Hamas or Israel move an inch to even start the process.

The viewpoints in this chapter do offer some plans. One wonders if Israel making a concerted effort to improve the lives of the Palestinians of Gaza can make a difference. Could that possibly shift them to the side of the Israelis given the view that Hamas embraces their suffering as a means of creating more friction? One wonders if simply allowing the Palestinians to leave Gaza would work given their strong belief that they belong there and opening up the borders to their departure would be tantamount to kicking them out of their homeland?

The suggestions here might or might not work. The authors that offer ideas that would aid all concerned—Israelis and Palestinians alike—bring greater validity to the table. But it has become painfully obvious that only through compromise, open minds, and a desire for peace on both sides can this complex problem be resolved.

> "*Outsiders do not have to choose either to side with Jews or to side with Palestinians. It is possible to listen to, hold compassion for, and support the human rights and safety of BOTH Jews and Palestinians.*"

Listen to Both Sides and Seek a Shared Future

Lisa Schirch

In the following viewpoint Lisa Schirch argues that while both Israel and Palestine each have their own narratives about their history, their claims, and their suffering, it is necessary to accept the truth of both sides in order to broker peace. The author also contends that western Christians must accept their own deep-seated historical role in the current Israeli-Palestinian crisis. Shirach serves as research director for the Toda Peace Institute in Tokyo and is a senior policy advisor at the Alliance for Peacebuilding in Washington, DC.

As you read, consider the following questions:

1. What does the author mean by a "shared future?"
2. How different are the Jewish and Palestinian narratives according to the viewpoint?
3. What is "spiritual nausea" as described by the rabbi quoted in the viewpoint?

"Two Peoples, One Homeland: Listening to Both Israel And Palestine," by Lisa Schirch. December 7, 2018. Reprinted by permission.

In May 2018, Jews in Israel celebrated the 70th anniversary of their fight for the creation of an independent state, and Palestinians marked 70 years of the loss of their homes, farms and villages resulting from that war. On May 14, 2018, the United States opened its controversial new embassy in Jerusalem to fanfare and applause from Jewish groups and their allies who want the world to recognize Jerusalem as the undivided capital of Israel. Meanwhile, on the same day, tens of thousands of Palestinians protested the *Nakba*, the catastrophe of losing their homes and villages, along the border fence separating Gaza and Israel. The Palestinian "Great March of Return" continued for six weeks as Gazans asserted their desire to return to their homes and protested the blockade of Gaza and the move of the US Embassy from Tel Aviv to Jerusalem. Most of the Palestinian protestors were nonviolent and included many women and children. Some Palestinians threw stones and Molotov cocktails and rolled burning tires at Israeli soldiers on the other side of the Gaza border. In response to the protestors, Israeli soldiers used live fire weapons, killing more than 100 and wounding more than 13,000 Palestinians.

Many Israelis and Palestinians are eager for outsiders to take their side, and to demonize the other side. There are few outsiders or insiders who can articulate the traumas and narratives of all sides involved. Any who mention any hint of compassion for one side are quickly labeled traitors by others. But any meaningful social change requires bringing justice, freedom and security for *all* sides.

This article lays out an approach that describes a solution not based on one side winning and one side losing. Instead, this article argues a win/win solution is possible, a *shared future* where Jews and Palestinians share the land they both call home. In order to arrive at a shared future, it is first necessary to listen closely to the narratives, needs and interests of all sides.

Jewish Narratives

A common Jewish narrative about the current conflict begins with Romans sending Jews into exile after the destruction of the Temple in Jerusalem in A.D. 70. For nearly two millennia, Jews prayed for and imagined their return to the land of Israel. After centuries of persecution and attempts to assimilate, the terror of the pogroms in Eastern Europe against both secular and religious Jews in the 1800s convinced many Jews to join the Zionist movement. Zionists argued that Jews had tried every other way to find their safety, and that the only way left for Jews to be safe was to create a Jewish state as a refuge from persecution. Zionists began immigrating to what was then called Palestine, where Palestinian Arabs and a small population of Jews lived.

Then came the Holocaust and tens of thousands of European Jewish refugees and more than 800,000 Jewish refugees from Muslim majority countries fled persecution. Hitler used propaganda in Arabic speaking countries, and some Muslim and Arab leaders participated in spreading antisemitism while others recognized the shared suffering of both Muslims and Jews. Many Jews saw no alternative but to flee from their homes. Many countries refused to take Jewish refugees. So many Jews fled to the newly created state of Israel, and fought to find land, homes, and farms and the newly created state of Israel.

Jewish narratives often point out that Israel is the only Jewish-majority country, and the only society that structures all of its social and cultural life around the Jewish religious calendar. Jews are a small minority in every other country where they live. According to the Pew Research Center, there are only 14 million Jews in a world of 2.2 billion Christians, 1.6 billion Muslims, 1 billion Hindus and nearly 500 million Buddhists.[1] There are 49 Muslim majority countries and 100 Christian majority countries. Some Jewish narratives also point out that while the creation of Israel happened at the expense of Palestinians, most other states in the world were also created by either forcibly converting Indigenous populations and using repression.

In this mainstream Jewish narrative, Israel is both a safe haven for Jews suffering persecution for millennia, and a Jewish return from exile to the promised land. For many Jews, the existence of Israel as a state holds significant importance to their ability to survive as a people. Many view both Western and Arab criticism of Israeli policies as simply an extension the desire to destroy Israel and a continuation of centuries of anti-Jewish violence. The Israeli government, mainstream media and Christian Zionists often portray Israeli policies as unquestionably noble and view Palestinians are viewed as Arabs (to delegitimize a Palestinian identity) and "terrorists" without any legitimate grievances.

Palestinian Narratives

A common Palestinian narrative of the conflict begins with a description of the *Nakba*, the catastrophe of Palestinians losing their homes, villages and farms in the 1948 war between Jews and Arabs. This war resulted in 800,000 Palestinians losing their homes. There are more than 50 Palestinian refugee camps scattered throughout the Middle East today where Palestinians continue to live in severe poverty with few rights. For Palestinians, the creation of the state of Israel came at their expense and has led to seven decades of suffering.

Many Palestinians point out that Israel has three different relationships with Palestinians. Twenty percent of Israel's citizens are Palestinians. They often describe themselves as living as second-class citizens in a country designed to serve Jewish citizens. Second, Palestinians that live in the West Bank face a range of challenges from Israeli military occupation, following the 1967 war that defined the territorial lines for what is now formally considered the state of Israel, and what is widely known as the occupied West Bank of the Jordan River. The Oslo Agreement separates the West Bank into Areas A, B, and C where Palestinians have different degrees of control over the land. Throughout all areas of the West Bank, Palestinians report regular takeovers of land by Jewish settlements, Israeli military seizure of land, bulldozing homes, detention, torture, violence, and other forms of repression and humiliation.

The third group of Palestinians lives in Gaza, a strip of land south of the Israeli city of Tel Aviv that is separate from the West Bank. Palestinians in Gaza experience the Israeli blockade which prevents the import of goods and severe restrictions on food, water, electricity and healthcare, leading to 40% unemployment and a humanitarian crisis with millions living in poverty trapped in a small area of land surrounded by the Israel. The Gazan leadership of Hamas launches rockets to kill Israeli civilians in surrounding towns with the explanation that these are revenge killings for Israeli military killing of Palestinians and that they will not stop until Israel allows Palestinian refugees from the 1948 war to return to their land.

Palestinians want an end to the Gaza siege, an end to the occupation of the West Bank, full and equal rights as citizens of Israel, and restitution or the right to return to their homes. Many narratives from Palestinians and other Arabs view Israel as an occupier and oppressor. Some go so far as suggesting Jews should have stayed in Europe, and that it is unfair that Palestinians must suffer because of what Europeans did to Jews. Some view Jewish concerns for safety and antisemitism as exaggerated or even made up and view Jews from Europe simply as white colonialists who have taken over their land.

Recognizing Truth in All Sides

There are key Jewish and Palestinian people who recognize the truth in the narratives of all sides. For example, Rabbi Hanan Schlesinger describes listening to and digesting the Palestinian story as a form of "spiritual nausea." Rav Hanan explains that spiritual nausea is the "gut wrenching re-examining of identity that one must go through while coming to terms with the fact that his or her truth is not the only truth." It refers to the spiritual process of finding room in one's own identity for the identity of the other, of expanding one's sense of justice and truth to embrace the other.

Two-State Solution

For decades, the two-state solution has been held up by the international community as the only realistic deal to end the Israeli-Palestinian conflict. Its basis is two separate states, Israel and Palestine, living peacefully side by side on the land between the western bank of the Jordan river and the Mediterranean Sea. This territory would be divided broadly along the pre-1967 armistice line or "green line" —probably with some negotiated land swaps. Jerusalem, which both sides want as their capital, would be shared.

Past negotiations have failed to make progress and there are currently no fresh talks in prospect. The main barriers are borders, security, Jerusalem, refugees, Israel's insistence on being recognised as a "Jewish state" and the Palestinians' political and geographical split between the West Bank and Gaza.

The Palestinians demand that the border of their new state should follow the green line, giving them 22% of their historic land. But Israel, which has built hundreds of settlements on the Palestinian side of the green line over the past 50 years, insists that most of these should become part of Israel—requiring a new border which would mean, according to critics, the annexation of big chunks of the West Bank. Land swaps could go some way to compensate but negotiations have stalled on this fundamental issue.

Israel wants assurances of its security behind whatever borders may be established in a two-state solution.

Jerusalem is another obstacle. Israel has said it cannot agree any deal which sees the city shared or divided between the two sides. The Palestinians say they will not cede their claim and access to their holy sites, all of which are located in East Jerusalem, on the Palestinian side of the green line.

The Palestinians have long insisted that refugees from the 1948 war and their descendants should have the right to return to their former homes, although many diplomats believe they would settle for a symbolic "right of return." Israel rejects any movement on this issue.

Israel insists that the Palestinians must recognise Israel as a "Jewish state." The Palestinians say this would deny the existence of the one in five Israeli citizens who are Palestinian.

"The Two-State Solution in the Middle East—All You Need to Know," by Harriet Sherwood, *Guardian* News and Media Limited, December 28, 2016.

Rav Hanan describes the giving up of the exclusivity of one story as "destabilizing and almost literally painful." But, he notes, "it is absolutely necessary for any progress towards real coexistence." Likewise, Palestinian leader Sami Awad has experienced a similar transformation when he had an opportunity to visit Auschwitz, the concentration camp where Jews were killed during WWII. Sami Awad says during this visit he recognized the incomprehensible suffering of Jews and recognized their need to have a secure home.[2]

Writing Western Outsiders into the Story

Western outsiders rarely take into account their own responsibility for the suffering of *both* Jews and Palestinians. Outsiders from Western countries are not mere observers of Israel and Palestine. Some Palestinians point out that "Jews were kicked out of Europe by Christians and landed on the heads of Palestinians."

Western Christians were not innocent bystanders during the rise of Hitler. Mainstream western Christianity was deeply antisemitic. It gave rise to Nazi racial science and a theology that viewed Hitler as a savior implementing a divine plan. Significant numbers of Christian theologians participated in racial theology that asserted "morals pass through blood" and justified antisemitism. Christians used Jewish slave labor and worked directly for the Nazi regime, overseeing and participating in the Holocaust. By contributing to the centuries of persecution of Jews and forcing hundreds of thousands of Jews to flee toward Palestine, Christians are in part responsible for the dispossession of first Jews from their homes in Europe and in turn Palestinians from their homes in Palestine.

Key Principles for Talking about Israel and Palestine

Outsiders do not have to choose *either* to side with Jews *or* to side with Palestinians. It is possible to listen to, hold compassion for, and support the human rights and safety of BOTH Jews and Palestinians. Here are some principles for talking about Israel and Palestine while acknowledging all sides.

1. Understand the history of all sides and their legitimate grievances.

2. Acknowledge that both Jews and Palestinians have had the experience of living as refugees.

3. Empathize with the trauma that both Jews and Palestinians experience.

4. Recognize the significance of the land for all sides, that both Jews and Palestinians view all of the land as their homeland, and thus a shared future requires compromise on all sides.

5. Acknowledge the right to peoplehood and self-determination for both Jews and Palestinians. Both groups have a unique history, a unique culture, and view themselves as a people.

6. Acknowledge wrongdoing on all sides. Both sides have had extremists who called for the total destruction of the other side. Both sides have taken actions that make a solution more difficult.

7. Recognize positive aspects of both Israeli and Palestinian society. Both Jews and Palestinians are more than their conflict. They deserve to be listened to and understood for the identity and culture outside of the conflict as well.

8. Identify power differences and "false equivalencies" on all sides. Palestinians and Israelis do not suffer equally under the current situation. Today, Palestinians are currently suffering far more. But throughout history, Jews have suffered far more deaths from persecution than Palestinians. Historically, Jews have not had political power. Today, Jewish Israelis have far more power than Palestinians, but are a minority in the wider, powerful Arab and Muslim world.

9. Recognize that antisemitism is both a reality, and a politically charged accusation that shuts down concern for Palestinians. The horrific history of antisemitism means

that for many Jewish people, any concerns or criticism of Israeli policies by Christians, Europeans, the UN and Arabs, including Palestinians, are viewed through the lens of historic antisemitism. The Israeli government criticizes opponents of its policies by calling anything critical of Israel as antisemitic. At the same time, there is real antisemitism in the world and advocates of Palestinian rights are sometimes antisemitic.

10. Recognize different meanings of Zionism. Misunderstandings and assumptions about the term Zionism are a significant block to progress. Many assume that Zionism refers to the military takeover of all of Palestine and to achieve a religious Zionism where "The Land of Israel belongs to the People of Israel." However, Rav Menachem Froman, a Jewish settler argued that this was incorrect. Instead, he argued, "the People of Israel belong to the Land of Israel." In this view, Jews should not militarily control all the land or push out Palestinians. Instead, Jews should seek to live with Palestinians and treat them with full dignity and respect.[3] Zionism has many different meanings. Zionism and Palestinian rights can co-exist if Jews and Palestinians both imagine a future where they live side by side and have equal rights and freedoms.

Recognizing the needs and interests of all sides is an important step in finding a lasting solution.

Two Peoples, One Homeland

There are a wide variety of possible solutions. Right now, there is one state, Israel. In the current situation, Israelis live with full rights and a government that represents them. Palestinians are suffering under the Gaza siege, occupation of the West Bank, and restrictions on their rights and freedoms. While a two-state solution with separate land and governments for Palestinians and Israelis is still supported by some, it is difficult to imagine how this would happen with hundreds of thousands of Jewish settlers living all over the West Bank, and little territory left for a Palestinian state.

A more hopeful option is some type of creative hybrid solution, sometimes referred to as "two states, one homeland" that would declare all of the land as Palestine and all of the land as Israel.[4] Simultaneously, both groups would achieve their greatest goal; the ownership and identity of their homeland. While there would be some territories governed by a Jewish government, and others governed by a Palestinian government, there would be coordination on many areas. This option would protect a Jewish state and its need for security while also allowing for recognition of Palestinian rights and freedoms. Regardless of the solution proposed, outsiders can best support a solution when we listen to a range of voices from all sides of the conflict and support their needs and interests for human rights, safety and peace.

Notes

1. Pew Research Center for Religion and Public Life. "The Global Religious Landscape." December 18, 2012.

2. Lisa Schirch. "Spiritual Nausea, Two States, One Homeland: New Insights from a Dialogue between Jewish Settlers and Palestinian Activists." Personal Blog. November 15, 2017. Accessed on December 1, 2018 at https://lisaschirch.wordpress.com/2017/11/15/spiritual-nausea-two-states-one-homeland-new-insights-from-a-dialogue-between-jewish-settlers-and-palestinian-activists/

3. Douglas Martin. Menachem Froman, Rabbi Seeking Peace, Dies at 68. New York Times. March 9, 2013.

4. For more information, see this website: http://www.alandforall.org/en. Accessed on December 1, 2018.

> "*The dramatic deterioration in the
> health and welfare of civilians in
> Gaza in recent years represents an
> entirely man-made, and entirely
> avoidable, humanitarian nightmare.
> This nightmare must end and the
> situation must be reversed—not as a
> concession to Hamas, but because it
> is the right thing to do, both morally
> and strategically.*"

Blockade Strategy Must Be Rethought

Lara Friedman

*In the following viewpoint Lara Friedman writes extensively and
negatively about the Israeli blockade of the Gaza Strip, citing her
views that it is inhumane, ineffective, and illegal. She contends that
not only does the blockade strengthen Hamas, but it weakens the
Israeli state and sways public opinion against the government and
its policies. She further offers that the blockade has been a tragedy
for the Palestinian people without bringing hope to them or the
possibility of a peaceful resolution. Friedman is the president of the
Foundation for Middle East Peace.*

"'Top 10 Reasons for Reassessing the Gaza Blockade Strategy," by Lara Friedman,
Americans for Peace Now, June 3, 2010. Reprinted by permission.

As you read, consider the following questions:

1. Can an author who seeks an immediate peace have a handle on the complexities of the situation?
2. What actions taken by the Israelis does the author consider to be inhumane?
3. In what way does the author believe that Israel is strengthening Hamas through the blockade?

In June 2007, as part of an effort to pressure Hamas and force it out of power, Israel clamped a tight blockade on Gaza. The blockade blocks the free movement of all goods and people into and out of the Gaza Strip. This blockade is carried out by Israel along its border with the Gaza Strip and along the shores of Gaza, and by Egypt, along its border with the Strip. The blockade has continued through the past three years, condoned and supported by the United States and the international community.

1. The blockade is ineffective as a security measure.

The primary rationale for the blockade has always been Israeli security—the legitimate Israeli desire to stop Gaza militants getting their hands on more weapons. But it hasn't worked. The blockade didn't bring about an end to rocket attacks. To the contrary, rocket attacks escalated following the implementation of this policy, culminating in the 2008-2009 Gaza War. And even if it can be argued that the blockade is hindering the flow of weapons into Gaza, it is clearly is not stopping this flow: with the flourishing tunnel traffic between Gaza and Egypt that has developed since the blockade was established, today Israel military experts believe that Hamas continues to obtain weapons with little difficulty.

2. The blockade is ineffective as an anti-Hamas tactic.

The other rationale for the blockade was Israel's goal of ousting Hamas from power. Here again, the blockade hasn't worked. To the contrary, it has played into Hamas's hands. Rather than the hoped-for groundswell of popular Palestinian action against Hamas' government, the blockade has helped Hamas strengthen its hold on Gaza. Gaza has turned into a society that is almost entirely dependent on foreign aid, with poverty rates are so high that the UN estimates that more than 60% of households are now food insecure. And because of the blockade, the local population blames Israel, not Hamas, for this.

3. The blockade is ineffective as a means of freeing captured Israeli soldier Gilad Shalit.

The government of Israel has the right—indeed, the obligation—to take measures to free its captured soldier Gilad Shalit. However, the blockade has clearly failed to achieve this goal. Worse yet, the blockade has more likely undermined the effort to free Shalit. Hamas used Israeli unwillingness to end the blockade as a pretext for refusing to free Shalit, after adding lifting the blockade to its list of demands - in addition to the release of hundreds of prisoners held by Israel - in exchange for releasing him. Meanwhile international support for Israel's legitimate grievance over the imprisonment of Shalit diluted by ever-growing concerns over the blockade's impact on the population of Gaza, including children, women, the sick, and the elderly.

4. The blockade is hurting the entire population of Gaza.

While Gazans are not dying of starvation or epidemics, there is a humanitarian crisis in the Gaza Strip. For the past three years, Israel has prevented the entry of all but a trickle of humanitarian goods into Gaza. Additional goods enter via hundreds of tunnels under the Gaza-Egypt border. While it is true that there are additional quantities of food entering Gaza, residents don't have money to buy it, because Israel blocks the passage of goods that could be used for economic activity, including raw materials, construction materials, and export of finished products. More than 80% of Gaza residents are dependent on cash assistance from international and/ or Islamic charities in order to survive, and a similar percentage are dependent on food assistance.

Ninety-percent of Gaza's factories have closed or are operating at 10% or less capacity. Construction projects, including those designed to repair the damage from the 2008-2009 military operation, are halted, except for private actors who use construction materials purchased from the tunnels and taxed by Hamas. Unemployment in Gaza hovers at around 40%. A combination of supply restrictions imposed by Israel and financial disputes between Hamas and the Palestinian Authority have restricted the supply of fuel needed to produce electricity, forcing power outages of approximately 8 hours per day throughout the Gaza Strip.

More than 90% of the water is unsuitable for drinking by World Heath Organization standards and must be treated. Patients requiring medical care not available in Gaza face delays and sometimes refusals to permit the referral to hospitals in Israel, the West Bank, or third countries. Medical students are not permitted to leave Gaza to obtain training or studies in the West Bank, and medical personnel are often prevented from attending training opportunities abroad, making it difficult to improve the standard of care.

The situation in Gaza has been called a crisis of dignity. One and a half million people are being kept on "life support"— prevented from engaging in dignified, productive work via a policy Israel characterizes as "economic warfare" designed to pressure the Hamas regime. Human rights organizations characterize it as collective punishment, because civilians are being punished for acts they did not commit.

Such a policy is fundamentally wrong and ultimately counterproductive. It is equally wrong and counterproductive for the U.S. to condone such actions. The dramatic deterioration in the health and welfare of civilians in Gaza in recent years represents an entirely man-made, and entirely avoidable, humanitarian nightmare. This nightmare must end and the situation must be reversed—not as a concession to Hamas, but because it is the right thing to do, both morally and strategically.

5. The blockade is actually strengthening Hamas.

As a result of the blockade, Gaza's civilians are suffering and its independent merchant class has been wiped out, while Hamas' hold over Gaza has been strengthened through the control of the smuggling tunnels. Outside of UN aid and the limited aid that Israel permits to pass through its crossing points, nearly all regular goods for Gaza must pass through Hamas-controlled tunnels, which today are the backbone of Gaza's pseudo-economy. Today Hamas is even taxing the goods that come through these routes, meaning that the blockade has indirectly become a source of income for the Hamas government.

6. The blockade has helped wipe out moderate opposition to Hamas within Gaza.

As a result of the blockade, Gaza's moderate middle class—the people who in the past traded with Israel and had regular relations with Israelis—has been wiped out politically and economically. While one rationale for the blockade was that it would cause the people to rise up against Hamas and in favor of the kind of more moderate leadership that exists in the West Bank, instead today the only real opposition to Hamas comes from foreign-inspired and foreign-funded Islamists who oppose Hamas for being too moderate.

7. The blockade undermines the domestic legitimacy of Palestinian President Abbas and Prime Minister Fayyad.

Some argue that lifting the blockade would deal a blow to the Fatah-run PA and its leaders, President Mahmoud Abbas and Prime Minister Salam Fayyad. This argument is facile.

Abbas and Fayyad continue to call for an end to the blockade. For the sake of their own credibility as well as for their claim to lead all the Palestinian people (not just the West Bank) Abbas and Fayyad cannot sit by quietly and acquiesce to a situation in which more than a million Palestinians suffer. Similarly, they know that the Gaza blockade is actually strengthening Hamas' hold on Gaza, while diminishing the influence of those Gazans who would traditionally have represented their own power base.

8. The blockade is a strategic liability for Israel.

The blockade is generating friction between Israel and its allies who are finding it difficult to defend the policy to their own citizens. Some of these allies have assisted Israel by financing UN aid to keep Gaza afloat.

Israel's relations with Egypt are also being strained. The Israel-Egypt peace treaty is a cornerstone of Israeli security policy. But Egypt has its own vital security interests in the Sinai-Gaza border—interests that it sees being trampled by Israel as the blockade continues.

The blockade negatively impacts the image of Israel internationally, providing ready ammunition for anti-Israel sentiment and campaigns and fueling efforts to charge Israeli officials in foreign courts with violating the Geneva Convention. Every student who cannot exit Gaza to study, every patient who cannot exit Gaza for medical care, every bride in the West Bank who is separated from her groom in Gaza due to Israel's refusal to permit travel between the West Bank and Gaza, every West Bank resident who is pointlessly deported to Gaza for having failed to change his or her address to the West Bank before 2000, when Israel stopped accepting changes to the Palestinian registry - each of these is one more self-inflicted Israeli wound in the propaganda battle over Israel's legitimacy.

Speaking a week before the Gaza flotilla debacle, Israeli Foreign Ministry spokesman Yigal Palmor reportedly said: "We can't win on this one in terms of PR. If we let them throw egg at us, we appear stupid with egg on our face. If we try to prevent them by force, we appear as brutes."

9. The blockade undermines Israel's legitimate claims to self-defense.

Hamas is a terrorist organization that has carried out horrific attacks on Israel. It refuses to clearly and unequivocally accept Israel's right to exist. Israel has serious and understandable concerns about the dangers posed by Hamas in Gaza, including the danger posed by the importation of weapons to Gaza and the firing of weapons from Gaza into Israel.

The blockade, however, is not an appropriate answer to these concerns, and the maintenance of the blockade has become a burden and a liability for Israel. Today Israeli military might is being used—whether in the context of the Gaza War or in the context of efforts to stop ships at sea—to preserve a blockade that itself has proven to be ineffective and increasingly difficult to defend morally.

Maintaining a blockade that is ineffective, and presenting it as an existential matter of self-defense, undermines Israel's claim that it is acting in self-defense. The international reaction to the recent Gaza flotilla debacle underscores this point, with few—even among defenders of Israel—viewing Israel's actions as a response to a credible threat to the homefront. The international backlash to the 2008–2009 Gaza War offers a further example: while it was true that Israel attacked after facing months of rocket attacks from Gaza, the war was almost universally understood in the context of the years of misery imposed on Gaza by Israel's blockade.

Israel lives in a tough neighborhood and there is a very real possibility that Israel will have to act in its legitimate self-defense in the future. Unfortunately, conflating self-defense with defense of a blockade that is increasingly ineffective and morally indefensible risks undermining Israel's position on the international arena. Israel can't afford to be perceived as not being credible in what it asserts as self-defense.

10. The continued maintenance of the blockade makes tragedies inevitable.

The roots of this week's disaster lie not in the actions of the flotilla's participants or the actions of the Israeli government. The roots of this disaster lie in the failure of the policy, initiated by Israel after Hamas took over Gaza in 2007 (and supported by the international community), to block the free movement of goods and people in and out of Gaza.

The Gaza blockade is untenable and increasingly indefensible given the humanitarian crisis that it has created, and given its contribution to Israel's increasing international isolation. An effective ban on imports and smuggling of arms into Gaza - both by land and by sea—can be established and sustained through an international regime without subjecting the entire population to misery, and without Israel adopting policies that are clear strategic liabilities.

The roots of this crisis—the blockade—cry out for serious attention, even before considering the tremendous public relations nightmare that the current situation poses for Israel. Because if we don't deal with the roots of this crisis, it is only a matter of time before Israel will face another challenge to the blockade, and will be faced with another set of bad choices dictated by what is at heart a misguided and faulty strategy.

> "I'm not saying that an economic solution will end the conflict, but the logic that was applied with the Americans' Marshall Plan following World War II should be applied here too: One should aid in the civil and economic rehabilitation of the enemy."

Look to the Marshall Plan as a Solution to the Gaza Crisis

Eran Yashiv

In the following viewpoint Eran Yashiv argues that there is a practical solution to the Gaza crisis. He believes that a concerted effort to improve the lives of the Palestinian people would serve to brighten the prospects for a lasting peace. The author cites the Marshall Plan instituted after World War II, which brought stability to European nations —even Germany—as a measuring stick for the potential success of such a plan. He states that the blockade has done nothing but worsen the situation and that Israel should take a more positive approach in its relationship with the Palestinians to achieve its goals. Yashiv is a professor of social sciences at Tel-Aviv University

"A Practical Solution to the Crisis in Gaza," by Eran Yashiv, *Haaretz* Daily Newspaper Ltd, June 6, 2018. Reprinted by permission.

As you read, consider the following questions:

1. How is the plan laid out by the author unique in comparison to the others in this resource?
2. Does the author believe the Palestinians should be treated better by the Israeli government?
3. Do you believe the author's idea has the potential to lead to a long-lasting peace?

The situation in Gaza is depressing, it's true. But rather than give in to despair, I would like to suggest a practical solution that could save us and the Gazans from the vicious cycle in which we are currently trapped.

This depressing situation has arisen in Gaza, and to a large degree in the West Bank too, because there is no significant force acting to improve conditions for the people. Hamas' main interest is in preserving its power while amassing firepower, and it is willing to sacrifice lives to this end. The Israeli government is not offering any original ideas, and is taking a fairly passive stance toward Gaza. It certainly isn't overly concerned with Gazans' welfare. Egypt is trying to minimize the damage from Gaza, and international organizations are working at the margins, on a small scale. From time to time, conferences are held about support for Gaza, but they are mostly for show. In the absence of an "unseen hand" that will bring real change, this trap will continue to exact a heavy price.

A practical solution exists, however, and it is even fairly simple and inexpensive. The Gaza Strip is not the focus of any religious-ideological dispute, and is not situated in a strategic location. Its fundamental problems are terrible overcrowding, extreme poverty and continuous destruction of infrastructure. As Emmanuel Sivan recently wrote (in *Haaretz* in Hebrew, May 18), this situation has been developing for more than 30 years. But it is now acute, because Gaza has become vulnerable to epidemics that could overwhelm its hospitals and to possible acts of despair.

There is a connection between this situation and the events of the past days and weeks—the clashes over the marches to the border fence and the round of fighting (rocket and mortar fire from Gaza and Israeli airstrikes in response). Israel is mistaken to think that military pressure will lead to a solution in Gaza. In the 11 years since Hamas came to power, the situation has only gotten worse, as has the negative reaction to Israel.

Israel has taken hardly any positive, constructive steps. Its responses have been to destroy infrastructure, tighten the blockade and use military firepower. I'm not saying that an economic solution will end the conflict, but the logic that was applied with the Americans' Marshall Plan following World War II should be applied here too: One should aid in the civil and economic rehabilitation of the enemy, and not only that of the allies (Germany received the third largest amount of American aid).

There are proposals, such as building an artificial island, that could bear fruit many years from now. But by then Gaza will have collapsed. Practical steps must be taken first before weighing the viability of such grandiose projects.

Much more modest proposals, like easing the blockade and the facilitating the transit of goods, are insufficient. This sort of thing is heard all the time from politicians and pundits, but Israel cannot easily implement these steps—and, in any case, they would be a mere drop in the sea, given the scale of the problems.

What solution would give incentives for greater calm and pave the way to a sustainable "hudna"—or long-term cease-fire? Israel could act behind the scenes to establish an international task force, without being part of it. This task force would bring together experts in fields like health and vital infrastructure and would include European countries acceptable to both sides (Britain, Germany and France, for example).

The task force's first objective would be to rebuild the health and sanitation systems in Gaza, improving water and sewage systems and ensuring that hospitals can function properly. These countries have a wealth of experience with such systems in large urban areas, so progress could be seen in six to eight months, and this would help alleviate the humanitarian crisis that fueled the recent violence.

If there were major construction projects underway on the Gaza side of the fence, the kind of protests we've seen lately would almost surely have been less massive. If the task force is successful, these countries could set up something akin to the European Bank for Reconstruction and Development to address infrastructure problems.

Such an international professional body could jumpstart a long list of short-range and long-range projects (like building an airport and developing the offshore gas field). As for the "security risks" involved, bear in mind that Hamas has already waged several rounds of warfare against Israel, fired rockets and dug tunnels despite the Israeli blockade of the past decade or more. Still, creative ways can be found to reduce these risks.

This task force could also ensure that the funds reach their intended target—not the Hamas leadership. The cost of such an economic effort - $1-4 billion per year for several years, in my estimation – is not high in international terms. Remember that the Gazan economy is relatively small with a limited capacity to absorb investment.

Several hurdles must be overcome in order to ensure the success of this plan. The Israeli public's feelings toward Gazans range from indifference to hatred. Politicians, who have no vision for the future, fan these feelings as they concentrate on getting elected or staying in power.

The military leadership, which sees the dangers directly, isn't built to provide such solutions. The army knows how to fight, not how to build health infrastructure.

Add to this the fact that the world isn't all that concerned with the problems of Gaza. There are so many disasters happening in the Middle East (in Syria, Yemen, as well as Iraq and Libya) that it's hard to know what can be done, and ultimately nothing is done.

It's heartbreaking to see Gazans' suffering while many in Israel and the world remain indifferent, when an applicable solution is within reach.

> *"Anybody who talks about Israel's 'security concerns' as if those concerns aren't real, isn't worth listening to."*

The Only Real Solution Is to Rid the Region of Hamas

Robert L. Wolkoff

In the following viewpoint Robert L. Wolkoff claims that it is Hamas that controls the situation in Gaza and that its threat to the Israeli state provides justification of force such as the blockade. He feels that the suffering of the Palestinian people is actually smiled upon by Hamas, which prefers that suffering because it strengthens the possibility of achieving the ultimate goal, the destruction of the Jewish state. The author goes on to make suggestions as to how to weaken or rid the region of Hamas. Wolkoff is a New Jersey rabbi who has published hundreds of articles and lectured around the world on topics of interest to Jewish people

As you read, consider the following questions:

1. Why does the author open with a story about a genie?
2. Does the author make a valid point in stating that Hamas needs the Palestinian people to suffer for political gain?
3. What is wrong with giving in to tantrums?

"How Do You Solve a Problem Like Gaza?" by Robert L. Wolkoff, *Times of Israel*, June 8, 2018. Reprinted by permission.

S o a guy finds a bottle on the beach, rubs it, and a genie comes out. "I'll grant you anything you want," says the genie. "Great," says the guy. "I have relatives in England, but I hate flying. Build me a bridge from here to England. "Are you crazy?" says the genie. "That's impossible. There's not enough concrete on the planet to do something like that. Please be more realistic." "Okay," says the guy. "Figure out what to do about Gaza."

The genie thinks for a few minutes and says, "Did you want two lanes or four?"

This joke came to mind when one of my congregants responded to my last blog post, about the legitimacy of Israel's self-defense during the recent Gaza riots. He agreed with the general principle, but pointed out correctly that Israel, rightly or wrongly, has policies that make the life of Gazans miserable. Was there nothing that could be done?

This is my response.

There has been a lot of talk about what to do for Gaza, but every choice involves a dizzying array of unintended consequences. It's a geo-political tea party that would drive the Mad Hatter crazy.

Look at the options:

There are those who aren't concerned about Israel's "security concerns," who suggest simply ending the Israeli blockade because "it's the right thing to do."

Go directly to war, do not pass go, do not collect anything but body bags.

This would enormously strengthen Hamas, which is explicitly genocidal. That alone makes it anything but "the right thing to do." And if that weren't enough, the Palestinian Authority (PA) would be fatally weakened in the West Bank. Simply put, anybody who talks about Israel's "security concerns" with scare quotes, as if those concerns aren't real, isn't worth listening to. For sure, Israel won't be listening to them, and we shouldn't either.

A variant on the theme is to loosen the blockade, but not end it altogether. The idea here is that since Israel knows how to handle the Hamas tunnels and the Hamas rockets, we should let the cement and pipes through in order to ease the suffering of the civilian population.

Only two problems: First, it won't ease the suffering of the civilian population, because Hamas needs the civilian population to suffer. Second, it is an open invitation to a truly right-wingnut government taking over in Israel. All you need is one rocket to hit one kindergarten with kids in it (not an empty one, as happened just last week, in spite of Iron Dome, etc.), and the government of "appeasers" falls. And if you think Netanyahu is really right-wing, just wait.

On the other end of the spectrum are those that say Israel should go back into Gaza, reoccupy every inch, go through every house, every tunnel, arrest or kill every terrorist, and "clean up the mess."

What could possibly go wrong?

This plan should go about as well as Afghanistan. Thousands of dead Israeli soldiers, tens of thousands of dead Palestinians, mostly civilians.

And the world will sit by passively, without any negative consequences for Israel.

Not.

But what of the massive civilian suffering, the "strangulation," the "open air prison"? Get real. After Operation Protective Edge in 2014, the Palestinians were offered $5.4 billion ("billion" with a b) for reconstruction. 90,000 homes have been rebuilt, along with hospitals, schools, etc.

Sure, Israel could do things like expand Gaza's fishing zone, or loosen up on Gaza exports, or allow more areas to be cultivated for agriculture (you, know, areas near the border fence next to the Israeli fields burned by those ever-innovative Palestinian youth with their flaming kites. Gee, those kids…).

I doubt, though, that people who claim they are ready to die because they have nothing to live for will change their minds because they can catch a few more fish. When you say you have "nothing to lose," it implies that if you did have something to lose, it would change your mind. But no economic relief is really going to matter when you are led by people whose idea of victory is standing on a pile of rubble and flashing a "v"-sign. If unemployment is approaching 50% in Gaza, it's because Hamas wants employment to approach 50% in Gaza. (In the meantime, another Israeli tech-whiz will sell his after-school garage project to Google for a billion dollars)

There have been calls to bring in the PA, which could then spearhead a massive reconstruction with the backing of the Arab world and leapfrog into an independent Palestinian state. All that would need to happen would be for Hamas to disarm.

Wait, what?

Disarm Hamas?! Weapons are to Hamas what blood is to the circulatory system. Proof that G-d has a sense of humor is the ironic fact that the Hebrew word for violence is…"hamas." That anyone would seriously raise this (non)possibility is a mark of the desperation of well-meaning people to find a solution—any solution—to the problem of Gaza. Even one that doesn't work.

An option already proposed by Israel would be to take five billion dollars, build an island with an airport and a seaport, linked to Gaza by a bridge. Israel would be responsible for security, but other than that it would be the Arab states, or the international community, that would have to carry the ball. Which is vaguely like asking someone if they would like cancer. Egypt, for one, wants absolutely nothing to do with Gaza. Neither do the Europeans, who would be in constant confrontations with Hamas. The only ones that would fall all over themselves to make a mark in Gaza are the Iranians, who see Gaza as a bridgehead in their drive to the Mediterranean.

That won't help.

An alternative to all of these political machinations is simply for Israel to use the same five billion dollars to pay Gazans to leave. It's a lot cheaper than tanks, and the fact is that almost all the water in Gaza is (and will remain) undrinkable, so Gazan society is already on the verge of collapse—and that doesn't take into account global warming and sea-level rise, which in a few decades will put much of Gaza under water, and make agriculture impossible. But, of course, anyone who even suggests such a thing would be accused of ethnic cleansing. Better to let the Palestinians suffer nobly.

Sure.

So what's to do? As long as Hamas is in power, and wants misery, there's going to be misery. So how do we a) alleviate the misery while simultaneously b) diminishing the power of Hamas?

Here's my two-part suggestion: 1. Israel should offer to let a select number of Gazan workers (say, 5,000 to start) into Israel. They should get paid exactly the same wages as Israelis doing the same job. The security procedures that will be put in place should be as streamlined and gentle (albeit necessarily thorough) as possible. Over time, the numbers could increase. 2. UNWRA funds should be systematically decreased in rough proportion to the wages being brought in by the workers.

Why is this a good idea?

1. Part one doesn't involve an intricate minuet among international players. Israel can just do it. Part two, which does, would get broad backing for purely economic reasons. Why should the international community pay welfare money when people are actually getting jobs that pay them far more?

2. Beside putting more money into the Gazan economy, and doing it on the individual level, it will remove the well-documented negative consequences of UNWRA welfare payments. These keep the Palestinians detached from the reality that real economics involve something other than endless declarations of hate for Israel.

3. If Hamas goes along with this, suddenly people really will have "something to live for." In fact, on an Israeli salary, they can live like kings in Gaza. A janitor in Israel earns

$1,500/month. Average wage in Gaza is about a quarter of that ($419), if you are in the lucky half of the population that has a job at all.

4. If Hamas, true to form, prefers to keep everyone miserable, and refuses to let people participate on grounds of "anti-normalization of the Zionist entity," then two things happen. First, Gazans will look at Hamas and say "Are you meshuga?" (not exactly, but you get the idea). "You're making us turn down a dream job so we can all starve in solidarity?" That's not going to make Hamas any more popular, and the overthrow of Hamas can't come soon enough (for Gazans themselves, not to mention the rest of us). Second, Israel will be able to look to the EU, the UN, and the rogues' gallery of NGO's and say, "What do you want from us? We offered to build a bridge, they offered to burn it down."

This is not a big step forward. No illusions there. But it is a small step, which, as regards Gaza, is a minor miracle. It could shake up the situation, creating more options for the future.

Alan Dershowitz likes to say that in Israel, the pessimist says "It can't possibly get worse," and the optimist cheerily answers, "Oh yes it can!" As bad as it is in Gaza—and it's bad—it could easily get worse. Much worse. War, of course, is worse. But even in the absence of war, Hamas can continue to retard the growth of Gaza for its propagandistic purposes—the political equivalent of a childhood temper tantrum.

And every parent knows that when you give in to tantrums, you create a monster.

> "*The world is weary of this unending occupation and of entrenched, callous disregard and hatred, one for the other. The status quo is anything but static. It is going wrong fast—increasing injustice for the Palestinians, storing up trouble for Israel's children, and causing grave concern here among those responsible for Britain's national security.*"

Peace Depends on a Two-State Solution

Vincent Fean

In the following viewpoint Vincent Fean contends that it is unlikely that the continuation of the current situation in Gaza will ever result in peace and that only a two-state solution can achieve that goal. He feels that Israel can live in peace if assurance of its existence is given and that the Palestinians can greatly improve their quality of life if their leadership indeed promises the safety of Israel. The author details the specifics of his plan to create a two-state solution and emphasizes its importance given the untenable situation as it stands, blockade and all. Fean is a former British consul general to Jerusalem.

"Only a Two-State Solution Will Bring Peace to the Middle East. Let's Help to Realise It," by Vincent Fean, *Guardian* News and Media Limited, January 13, 2017. Reprinted by permission.

As you read, consider the following questions:

1. What is a two-state solution?
2. Does the author offer an opinion on Israel's potential survival if the Palestinians are allowed sovereignty?
3. What possibility does the author see for a peaceful solution considering the circumstances as they stood when he wrote this viewpoint?

I t's time that a decision was made as to whether Israel and Palestine can live side by side. Without change soon, the option will not be there. Israel's 50-year military occupation of Palestinian territory harms us all. The British minister for the Middle East, Tobias Ellwood, has deemed it "unacceptable and unsustainable."

Hope of change came when the UN security council, after eight years of silence, adopted a resolution with strong UK support once more condemning Israeli illegal settlements in the West Bank and East Jerusalem, and when the US secretary of state, John Kerry, set out his framework for a just peace. This Sunday, France will host an international conference seeking an equitable basis for ending the occupation.

Our prime minister, Theresa May, is a firm friend of Israel. Friends should tell each other the truth. Already, Israel's prime minister, Benjamin Netanyahu, has rejected the resolution, bizarrely accused Kerry of anti-Israel bias, and dismissed the Paris conference without bothering to await its outcome. In truth, this is disregard for the law, and the express will of the international community. So systematic settlement expansion, demolition of Palestinian homes and the closure of Gaza are set to continue in this low intensity, asymmetrical Israel/Palestine war.

The world is weary of this unending occupation and of entrenched, callous disregard and hatred, one for the other. The status quo is anything but static. It is going wrong fast—increasing injustice for the Palestinians, storing up trouble for Israel's children, and causing grave concern here among those responsible for Britain's national security.

Netanyahu has ignored the advice of his own law officer by supporting unprecedented Knesset legislation which would legalise most of the 100 settler outposts in the Palestinian West Bank, hitherto illegal even under Israeli law. If that bill passes, Britain and our partners will need to respond decisively to an act designed to prevent the solution of two states long espoused by both peoples—Israeli and Palestinian—and by us. Kerry called the one state outcome "separate and unequal"—apartheid by my definition, inevitably provoking chronic violence.

Indiscriminate Palestinian violence is morally wrong and futile, whether labelled terrorism or resistance. The Palestinians should be pressed to reunite on the basis of Palestine Liberation Organisation principles, first among them the recognition of the state of Israel on pre-1967 borders, done by Yasser Arafat in 1993 and reaffirmed by Mahmoud Abbas. Elections are overdue in Gaza, the West Bank and East Jerusalem, the occupied Palestinian territories recognised as the state of Palestine by over 130 countries—although not yet by the UK.

This conflict is emphatically not between equals, but between the occupier and the occupied. Israel is creating new facts on the ground "leading towards one state and perpetual occupation" as Kerry warned. Before asking what Britain can do now to promote a just peace, it is worth saying what won't work. Quiet diplomacy, for one. We've tried that. Quiet diplomats get ignored. Second, US-led shuttle diplomacy, such as Kerry conducted for nine months. The US is necessary but not sufficient to resolve this conflict. And while no one can be sure what hand President Trump will play, the omens are bad.

And we can't leave it to the two conflicting parties to sort it out. The Middle East peace process became just that—a process. Direct unconditional negotiations between the strong and the weak only leave the weak, weaker. That's not how to end the occupation.

It will need an initiative by the international community, shaping the outcome, providing security guarantees, upholding the law, ensuring a better tomorrow for both peoples. The Paris conference should develop a wider consensus based on security council resolution 2334 and re-commit all Arab states to recognising Israel in return for a sovereign Palestine.

It is not enough to offer more carrots to both parties, hoping that both will bite. Israel has had a surfeit of carrots over the decades. Incentives to the Palestinians are contingent on ending the occupation—which only Israel can do.

So there are two things Britain should do. They go together. First, recognise the state of Palestine on 1967 borders now, or as soon as the Knesset "legalises" outposts, in breach of international humanitarian law; and secondly uphold that law without fear or favour—with serious consequences for whoever breaks it.

British recognition of Palestine acknowledges the Palestinian right to self-determination, affirmed by the UK 18 years ago at the Berlin European council. Far from delegitimising Israel, it reaffirms our 1950 recognition of Israel on the borders created two years before, unless both parties agree to any change. I commend a petition asking our government to recognise Palestine.

If we mean what we say about two states, we need to will the means. By recognising both states in the two-state solution, we legitimise both. Affirming the equal rights of both peoples is consistent with our values and in our national interest. One state— separate and unequal—would be unjust, unstable and violently divisive: an avoidable disaster for Israelis, Palestinians and us. Five years ago, the then foreign secretary William Hague said: "We reserve the right to recognise a Palestinian state bilaterally at a moment of our choosing and when it can best help bring about peace". I've said it before, but never has it been more true—now is the time.

> *"Prime Minister Netanyahu had
> said the two-State solution was now
> behind him"*

The Two-State Solution Is the Only Way Out

United Nations General Assembly

In the following viewpoint the United Nations emphasizes the need for a two-State solution to the Middle East crisis. The possibility of a two-State solution was discussed at a meeting held in Moscow in 2015, which certainly did not result in any tangible progress. But the notion of a separate Palestinian state has not been diminished by the lack of success in getting it accomplished and the unwillingness of both Hamas and the Israeli government to embrace the idea. The United Nations expressed an understanding that only through serious negotiations and a willingness to consider such a plan can a two-state solution be achieved. The United Nations is responsible for maintaining international peace and security.

As you read, consider the following questions:

1. What did the secretary-general conclude?
2. How well does this viewpoint explain the need for a two-State solution?
3. What is BDS?

From "Two-State Solution Only Viable Way to Resolve Israeli-Palestinian Conflict, Secretary-General Tells International Meeting as It Opens in Moscow" by General Assembly, July 1, 2015. ©2015 United Nations. Reprinted with the permission of the United Nations."

As a vicious tide of terror and extremism swept the Middle East, the international community must stay focused on resolving the Israeli-Palestinian conflict and the two-State solution as the only viable way to make that happen, United Nations Secretary-General Ban Ki-moon said in his message to the United Nations International Meeting in Support of Israeli-Palestinian Peace, which opened this morning in Moscow.

"It will demand difficult decisions from both parties. However, it is precisely because of the dangers that lurk in the Middle East today that both sides must show leadership and personal commitment to peace and negotiations," Mr. Ban said in a message delivered on his behalf by Nickolay Mladenov, United Nations Special Coordinator for the Middle East Peace Process.

The two-day meeting, convened under the theme "The two-State solution: a key prerequisite for achieving peace and stability in the Middle East" by the Committee on the Exercise of the Inalienable Rights of the Palestinian People, aimed to mobilize support for a just and comprehensive solution to the question of Palestine. It will explore ways to foster the conditions needed for a successful political process and review international efforts to achieve the two-State solution—including those within the framework of the Arab Peace Initiative, the Quartet, the League of Arab States, the Organization of Islamic Cooperation (OIC) and other multilateral organizations—as well as in the context of the United Nations.

Israel's nearly half century-long occupation must end and failure to do so could further destabilize the region, Mr. Ban warned. Despite setbacks over the years, most people on both sides still supported the idea of two States—Israel and Palestine—living side by side. "It is their voices we must listen to, and their efforts we must support," he said.

The Secretary-General welcomed Israeli Prime Minister Benjamin Netanyahu's recent statements supporting the two-State concept and said he had written to the Prime Minister to encourage him to take concrete, credible steps—including a freeze on illegal settlement building and planning, which made a final agreement more difficult, if not impossible—in order to jumpstart meaningful negotiations. Politicians on both sides should refrain from provocative actions and rhetoric and they must build upon existing agreements, including relevant Security Council resolutions, the road map and the Arab Peace Initiative, to advance a final status accord.

He said the Palestinian Government should be fully empowered to assume responsibility for Gaza's governance and security, including control of the enclave's border crossings into Israel. He also expressed worries over the recent resumption of rocket attacks on Israel by Palestinian militants in Gaza, stressing that all factions on the ground were responsible for keeping the peace in Gaza and preventing the escalation of violence.

Mr. Ban pledged to work with all parties to foster a return to peace talks and encouraged the Quartet—comprising the United Nations, Russian Federation, United States and the European Union—as well as the Arab League, the OIC, and regional and international stakeholders to play a more active, supportive role.

In addition to Mr. Ban's statement, this morning's session also heard from Alexander Pankin, Director of the Department of International Organizations at the Russian Ministry of Foreign Affairs; Fodé Seck (Senegal), Chairman of the Committee on the Exercise of the Inalienable Rights of the Palestinian People; Riad Malki, Minister for Foreign Affairs of the State of Palestine; and Nabil Elaraby, Secretary-General of the League of Arab States.

Mr. Pankin (Russian Federation) said that his country would do its part in international forums, particularly the Quartet. His Government had always been in favour of a just, comprehensive settlement, in line with all relevant General Assembly and Council resolutions, as well as the Arab Peace Initiative. The peace process should ensure the creation of an independent, viable Palestinian State co-existing peacefully alongside Israel, he said, expressing hope that Mr. Netanyahu's statements last month supporting the two-State solution would be followed by practical steps for implementation.

The Russian Government, he said, firmly supported all efforts to unify the Palestinian people, particularly as Palestine's national sovereignty would contribute to peace and stability not only with Israel, but also in the wider region. Turning to Gaza and expressing concern over the grave humanitarian situation there, he called for steps aimed at removing Israel's blockade of the coastal strip and stressed the important role of donor countries in financing its reconstruction and, in that connection, the international donor conference on the matter, held in Cairo in October 2014.

Mr. Seck, Chair of the Palestinian Rights Committee, noted that last year the breakdown of negotiations and the ensuing violence culminated in one of the deadliest wars in Gaza, leaving more than 2,100 Palestinians dead and 100,000 homeless. Amidst an almost complete blockade, reconstruction had barely begun and would take years. Settlement construction, land confiscation, housing demolitions and violence in the West Bank were ongoing. The Israeli Government's statements following elections there in March raised questions over its commitment to the two-State solution.

Still, there was a new international awareness that the situation could not continue and that there was no "freezing of the conflict," he said. The Committee welcomed recent efforts to rescue the two-State solution, notably by the European Union, the League of Arab States follow-up committee of foreign ministers and France's initiative for a Security Council resolution calling for a final status agreement within 18 months—and to involve more actors in the process. The Committee was also encouraged by the establishment last week of relations between the State of Palestine and the Vatican—the 136th State to recognize Palestine.

But Mr. Malki, Foreign Minister of Palestine, said many in the international community had turned their focus away from the Israeli-Palestinian conflict towards other conflicts in the region.

And for its part, Israel had never shown a real commitment to the two-State solution. The 1993 Oslo Accords signed by Israel and the Palestine Liberation Organization (PLO) were supposed to lead to a comprehensive peace agreement—ensuring an end to the Israeli occupation and creation of a sovereign Palestinian State—by May 1999. Instead, Israel had continued violating international law and pushing the Palestinians further and further away from independence.

During Israel's 2014 attack on Gaza, entire Palestinian families were decimated, while more than 140 lost three or four family members, he said. Israel targeted civilian infrastructure, including schools of the United Nations Relief and Works Agency for Palestine Refugees in the Near East (UNRWA) where families had sought shelter, depriving Palestinians of any safe haven. Jerusalem had been the primary target of the forcible transfer of Palestinians out of, and Israelis into, the territory.

"Both are war crimes under the Rome Statute. The settlement regime is ever growing, thus shrinking by the hour the prospects for peace," he said, adding that escalating attacks against holy sites aimed to transform a political conflict into a religious one, driving the region further down a frightening path.

Amid such formidable obstacles, he said, the Palestinian people were determined to achieve their inalienable rights, live in freedom and dignity, and take their rightful place among the world's free nations. It was time for the world to recognize the State of Palestine, hold Israel accountable for its offenses and set up an international mechanism to monitor both sides' compliance with a final peace agreement.

"It is either a two-State solution on the 1967 borders or an apartheid reality the world cannot tolerate," he said, adding that "for those who call on us to be patient and continue to reject international intervention, in violation of their own obligations under international law, we say: if they are waiting for the right time to intervene, our freedom and independence are long overdue."

The State of Palestine was charting a new peace offensive, he went on. Granted observer State status in the United Nations in November 2012, and recognized by the Vatican last week, it was now seeking the recognition of more States. It also was pushing for a new framework for peace and the establishment of clear terms of reference, a timetable for a final status agreement and an international monitoring mechanism to ensure accountability. He welcomed France's initiative for a Council resolution calling for those parameters. Impunity was a tremendous obstacle to peace. The State of Palestine had chosen justice rather than vengeance, and, as such, it was also seeking accountability through the International Criminal Court, the Human Rights Council and the Conference of the High Contracting Parties of the Geneva Conventions.

He also implored European Union members to uphold the commitments they had made in 1999, following the signing of the Oslo peace agreements, when they affirmed their intention to recognize the State of Palestine in due time. How then, 15 years later, had a majority of European Union member States, including all those that adopted the Berlin Declaration, with the important exception of Sweden, decided not to recognize State of Palestine? he asked. "If they are conditioning recognition on the results of negotiations, we assure them that our right to self-determination and freedom is not negotiable and that support for a sovereign State of Palestine on the 1967 borders is the best antidote to settlement activities."

Mr. Elaraby, Secretary-General of the Arab League, said the real way to end the conflict was to end the occupation and conclude a final status agreement and not simply manage the conflict—a process that had enabled Israel to continue to delay peace talks while grabbing more land. "Israel is the only country in the world that thinks that time is a strategic objective," he said, stressing that the international community must actively apply pressure on that nation and adopt serious positions to combat Israeli violations and policies, rather than just issuing condemnations.

Israel, which believed it was above the law, was sponsoring the "last outpost of apartheid in the twenty-first century," he said. But instead of putting an end to Israel's arrogance, the international community had turned a blind eye, causing the conflict to fester and risk going beyond the Middle East to shake the foundations of the current world order, while encouraging the illegal use of force. Israel could become a law-abiding State and comply with Security Council resolution 1397 (2002), which affirmed the two-State solution. But Israel's flippant disregard had rendered the resolution impotent. Moreover, Prime Minister Netanyahu had said the two-State solution was now behind him, affirming that Israel only wanted to continue occupying Palestinian land and to have futile negotiations.

He said the Security Council must take the necessary measures to make the two-State solution a reality, by implementing its resolutions, including 242 (1967), which called for Israel's full withdrawal from all occupied Arab territories, and 338 (1973), which reaffirmed resolution 242 (1967) and called for a ceasefire agreement. Furthermore, it must adopt a binding resolution, under Chapter VII of the United Nations Charter, and States must implement it. In that regard, he urged full support for the text tabled by France for a Council resolution setting well-known terms of reference, a mechanism for implementation and a complete halt of settlement activity.

Also needed was a serious, effective and urgent review of the role of the Quartet, which, despite the hopes attached to it, had not accomplished a single thing on the ground in 10 years, he said. The Security Council had not given it a clear mandate, leaving it to focus on conflict management. Resorting to the International Court of Justice, which had issued a landmark advisory opinion, and now the International Criminal Court were important options. In addition, the growing Boycott, Divestment, and Sanctions Movement, known as BDS, had indeed started to affect the Israeli economy, as had the European Union's guidelines that it label products made in the settlements. Those movements should be expanded.

Statements

The representative of Egypt said implementation of the Arab Peace Initiative remained subject to serious negotiations. An end to unilateral measures carried out by Israel, its blockade of Gaza and its seizure of East Jerusalem was needed, as was the implementation of the "land for peace" principle and the adoption of positions conducive to launching peace talks. Egypt was doing its part, he said, noting that at present it led OIC efforts by chairing that body's third meeting of the Ministerial Contact Group on Defending the Cause of Palestine and Al-Quds Al-Sharif, and the Arab Ministerial Committee. Egypt also hosted the international donor conference in October 2014 on Gaza reconstruction and contributed to efforts to unite the Palestinian parties. So long as Israel continued to occupy Palestinian territory, the Middle East would never achieve the peace desired.

Venezuela's representative condemned Israel's colonial practices against the Palestinian people, and asked how much longer the Palestinian people would have to endure suffering. In view of the continuous violations of international law, perpetrators must be brought to justice. The International Criminal Court's recent recognition of Palestine as a member was a step in the right direction. The Court should put an end to impunity in the Occupied Palestinian Territory. Thus far no one had been held responsible for Israel's deadly "Operation Protective Shield." On the contrary, two weeks ago an Israeli court acquitted those responsible for killing four Palestinian children playing soccer on a beach in Gaza. He reaffirmed Venezuela's firm support for the Palestinian people's right to self-determination, France's initiative in the Council and the Arab Peace Initiative.

The representative of South Africa said her country's freedom would never be complete as long as its brothers and sisters in the Occupied Palestinian Territory were not free. South Africa understood first-hand the pain of a people under occupation, most of whom lived below the poverty line. South Africa's democracy was obtained through inclusive negotiations with all political parties. Israelis and Palestinians, with the international community's full support, could jointly craft a workable two-State solution. South Africa was doing its part, having appointed special envoys to assist that process. To make progress on basic issues that had been stumbling blocks in the past, all Palestinian parties and factions must form a collective solidarity front for negotiations; the blockade of Gaza must be lifted, settlement construction must end, and there must be a just solution to the Palestinian refugees' plight.

Jordan's representative said the creation of an independent Palestinian State living in peace and security was a top priority for his Government. All the independent reports of the gravely unjust living conditions of the Palestinian people must serve as alarm bells for change and serious, productive, internationally monitored negotiations. The parties must refrain from unilateral measures that would undermine the peace process. Jordanian diplomacy would always support peace until the Palestinians were given the security, dignity and independent State they deserved, and until they played their rightful role in the Middle East. Jordan would keep the channels of communication open with all international parties to achieve those goals.

Indonesia's representative called on the Security Council to stop being on the sidelines of international peace efforts and to shoulder its responsibility. Indonesia's support for the Palestinian people was strong and unwavering. He endorsed any proposal to foster talks between the two parties, including the proposal for an international conference in Paris. Double standards in the current peace process must end. Support must be strengthened for more robust participation of the State of Palestine in the Middle East arena. The recent establishment of diplomatic relations between Palestine and the Vatican opened an opportunity for the latter to strengthen support for Palestine among the world's 1 billion

Catholics. He welcomed the recent publication of the report of the Commission of Inquiry investigating Israel's 2014 conflict in Gaza and encouraged Palestinians to use it in international courts to demand that Israel be held to account.

Morocco's representative said his Government had espoused the Palestinian cause and made it a top priority. Morocco's King had chosen to contribute to social and education projects for the benefit of the Palestinian people, and was sponsoring field projects to help Jerusalemites preserve their religious and cultural landmarks in the face of the Judaization of the city. The international community must launch a new dynamic that would serve as a catalyst for the peace process, culminating in the creation of an independent Palestinian State, with East Jerusalem as its capital. Any attempt to promote a fait accompli of just one State in the region would only lead to a feeling of injustice among Palestinians.

The representative of China reaffirmed his Government's support for a peaceful settlement to the question of Palestine. Over the years, it had provided financial and humanitarian aid to the Palestinian Authority. China had joined global efforts to help Israel and Palestine put an end to the spiral of violence and to resume negotiations. He expected the United Nations to heed the just calls of the Palestinian people, and to the Arab States to help end the occupation and rebuild Gaza.

Pakistan's representative said the on-again, off-again negotiations had not produced anything concrete. Talks for the sake of talks were neither sustainable nor acceptable. Illegal settlements were eating away at prospects for peace. The two-State solution was the goal that the international community must uphold. A one-State reality would be disastrous not only for the Palestinians but also for the wider region. It was high time for the Security Council to assume its responsibility and adopt a resolution that would set a clear timeline for creation of an independent Palestinian State and an end to the occupation.

Periodical and Internet Sources Bibliography

The following articles have been selected to supplement the diverse views presented in this chapter.

Hady Amr. "Gaza—Is there a fix? Brookings, December 5, 2017. https://www.brookings.edu/blog/markaz/2017/12/05/gaza-is-there-a-fix.

Zack Beauchamp. "What are the 'Two-State Solution' and 'One-State Solution"? Vox, May 14, 2018. https://www.vox.com/2018/11/20/18080094/what-are-the-two-state-solution-and-the-one-state-solution.

Ron Ben-Yishai. "There Is a Way to Solve the Gaza Crisis." YNet, May 21, 2018. https://www.ynetnews.com/articles/0,7340,L-5266644,00.html.

Ben Glaze. "How to Solve the Gaza Problem? Six Experts Tell Us How They Would Bring Peace." *Mirror*, August 3, 2014. https://www.mirror.co.uk/news/world-news/how-solve-gaza-problem-six-3958168.

International Crisis Group. "Averting war in Gaza." International Crisis Group, July 20, 2018. https://www.crisisgroup.org/middle-east north-africa/eastern mediterranean/israelpalestine/b60-averting-war-gaza.

Jerusalem Post Staff "Six Ways to Solve the Crisis in Gaza." *Jerusalem Post*, June 10, 2018. https://www.jpost.com/Arab-Israeli-Conflict/Six-ways-to-solve-the-crisis-in-Gaza-559624.

Avi Melamed. "A Realistic Solution to the Israeli-Palestinian Conflict." Forbes, April 5, 2016. https://www.forbes.com/sites/realspin/2016/04/05/a-realistic-solution-to-the-israeli-palestinian-conflict/#6d4d12427631.

For Further Discussion

Chapter 1

1. Did Israel have the right to claim Gaza based on its roots and need for a homeland to guard against persecution?
2. Based on the articles provided, do you believe Israel has taken a humanitarian approach to its treatment of Palestinians in Gaza?

Chapter 2

1. Can you envision any ending to the Gaza blockade through international legal channels?
2. Has the United Nations taken a strong enough stand for or against the blockade in an attempt to end the crisis?
3. What are some of the legal considerations cited in the articles from this chapter that help determine right and wrong?

Chapter 3

1. Why do you feel or not feel that the Israeli treatment of the Palestinians in Gaza constitutes a crime against humanity?
2. Can the propaganda on one side be believed more than the other based on freedoms of speech and press philosophies embraced by Hamas and Israel?

Chapter 4

1. Can the Israeli government institute any improvements to its treatment of the people in Gaza that would still ensure its right to exist?
2. How have Palestinian protests and violence on both sides affected opportunities for a solution?
3. Must the United States become more strongly involved in negotiating a settlement that would end the blockade?

Organizations to Contact

The editors have compiled the following list of organizations concerned with the issues debated in this book. The descriptions are derived from materials provided by the organizations. All have publications or information available for interested readers. The list was compiled on the date of publication of the present volume; the information provided here may change. Be aware that many organizations take several weeks or longer to respond to inquiries, so allow as much time as possible.

American Ethical Union

2 West 64th Street
New York, NY, 10023
(212) 873-6500
website: www.aeu.org

An ethical society is a community of people dedicated to improving lives in the United States and around the world through greater humanity and ethics. Its foundation is a belief that all people have worth and that life is sacred, interrelated, and interdependent. The organization boasts member groups throughout America.

Americans for Peace Now

2100 M Street NW, Suite 619
Washington, DC, 20037
(202) 408-9898
website: www.peacenow.org

The mission of Americans for Peace Now is to educate and persuade the American public and its leadership to support and adopt policies that will lead to comprehensive, durable, Israeli-Palestinian and Israeli-Arab peace, based on a two-state solution, while ensuring the existence of Israel.

American Society of International Law

2223 Massachusetts Avenue
Washington, DC, 20008
(202) 939-6001
website: www.asil.org

The American Society of International Law has been in existence for more than one hundred years. It was chartered in 1950 by the United States Congress to further the study of international law and promote the establishment and maintenance of international relations between people and countries based on law and justice.

Amnesty International

5 Penn Plaza, 16th Floor
New York, NY, 10001
(800) AMNESTY
website: www.amnestyusa.org

Amnesty International USA seeks to engage people in the United States to fight injustice throughout the world while doing the same to protect the rights of the American people as well. The organization boasts more than one million members in the United States who are part of a larger global movement of more than seven million in 150 countries.

Brookings Institution

1775 Massachusetts Avenue NW
Washington, DC, 20036
(202) 797-6000
website: www.brookings.edu

The Brookings Institution is a nonprofit public policy organization that has more than one hundred years of history behind it. Its mission is to conduct in-depth research that leads to new ideas for solving problems both nationally and internationally, including those in the Middle East.

Committee for Accuracy in Middle East Reporting in America (CAMERA)

(617) 789-3672

website: www.camera.org

email: https://www.camera.org/about/contact-us

Perceived inaccuracy and bias in the reporting of news about the Middle East inspired the creation of this organization. The Committee for Accuracy in Middle East Reporting in America works through media-monitoring and research to promote accurate and balanced coverage of Israel and its relationships with the Palestinians and other nations of the region.

Human Rights Watch

350 Fifth Avenue

New York, NY, 10118-3299

(212) 290-4700

website: www.hrw.org

This nonprofit organization promotes human rights around the world with a staff of global experts, lawyers, journalists, and academics of diverse nationalities. Its reports on human rights abuses and meets with governments as well as regional groups to improve the lives of those in the international community.

Institute for Middle East Understanding

2913 El Camino Real, #436.

Tustin CA, 92782

(718) 514-9662

website: www.imeu.org

email: info@imeu.org

This independent nonprofit organization provides journalists quick access to information about Palestine and the Palestinians, as well as expert sources in the United States and in the Middle East. It works with journalists to increase the public's understanding about the socioeconomic, political, and cultural aspects of Palestine, Palestinians, and Palestinian Americans.

Bibliography of Books

Vittorio Arrigoni. *Gaza: Stay Human*. Markfield, UK: Kube Publishing, 2010.

Phyllis Bennis. *Understanding the Palestinian-Israeli Conflict: A Primer*. New York, NY: Olive Branch Press, 2015.

Ian Carroll. *Israel and Palestine: The Complete History*. Dark River Publishing, 2018.

Jimmy Carter. *Palestine: Peace, Not Apartheid*. New York, NY: Simon & Schuster, 2007.

Joyce Chediac. *Gaza: Symbol of Resistance*. New York: World View Forum, 2011.

Noam Chomsky and Ilan Pappe. *On Palestine*. Chicago, IL: Haymarket Books, 2015.

Norman Finkelstein. *Gaza: An Inquest Into Its Martyrdom*. Oakland, CA: University of California Press, 2018.

Daniel Gordis. *Israel: A Concise History of a Reborn Nation*. New York, NY: Ecco Publishing, 2016.

Yassi Klein Halevi. *Letters to My Palestinian Neighbor*. New York, NY: Harper, 2018.

Jeremy R. Hammond. *Obstacle to Peace: The U.S. Role in the Israeli-Palestinian Conflict*. Terrace, FL: Worldview Publications, 2016.

Donald Macintyre. *Gaza: Preparing for Dawn*. London, UK: Oneworld Publications, 2017.

Ilan Pappe. *The Ethnic Cleansing of Palestine*. London, UK: Oneworld Publishing, 2007.

Melissa Rossi. *What Every American Should Know About the Middle East*. New York, NY: Plume Publishing, 2008.

Ari Shavit. *My Promised Land: The Triumph and Tragedy of Israel*. New York, NY: Spiegel & Grau, 2013.

Index

A

Abbas, Mahmoud, 20, 53, 56, 57, 139–140, 155
American Family News Network, 53–57
Americans for Peace Now, 135–142
American Society of International Law, 83–91
Amnesty International, 80, 81, 102–113
Arab League, 51, 117, 159, 162
Arafat, Yasser, 37, 48, 49, 61, 155
Argov, Shlomo, 33
Australian Financial Review, 58–61
Awda, Al-, 71, 74
Azaria, Elor,111

B

Balfour Declaration, 45
Barak, Ehud, 48, 49
Bar-Lev, Haim, 31
Begin, Menachim, 30
Ben-Gurion, David, 27, 44, 45, 47, 48
Blair, Tony, 110

C

Carter, Jimmy, 38
Clinton, Bill, 48, 49, 51, 61
Cohn, Marjorie, 95–101
Committee for Accuracy in Middle East Reporting in America, 65–69
conscientious objectors, to mandatory military service in Israel, 113

D

Dalloul, Motasem, 70–74
Deir Yassin massacre, 28

E

Egypt, 21, 29, 30, 31, 36, 47, 56, 60, 78, 81, 101, 105, 115, 117, 119, 136, 137, 140, 144, 150, 164
Ehrenfeld, Sylvain, 41–52
Ethical Culture Society of Bergen County, 41–52

F

Fatah, 54, 55, 60
Fean, Vincent, 153–156
Foreign Policy Journal, 23–40
Freedom Flotilla, 71–72, 80–81, 119, 140
Friedman, Lara, 135–142

G

Gaza Strip blockade
   as act of aggression, 23–40, 41–52
   as inhumane, 93–122
   legality of, 63–92
   possible solutions, 123–167
   as preservation of Israel, 19–22, 41–52, 53–57, 58–62
Gaza War, 136, 141
Geneva Conventions, 72, 81, 84, 97, 100, 140, 162
Greenblatt, Jason, 115
Guardian, 110–111, 130, 153–156
Gulf War, 47

H

Haaretz, 114–117, 143–146